A Prophet's Memoir

Sandra K. Blue

The birthing of a prophet will be the subtitle.

Copyright © 2023 by Sandra K. Blue

All rights reserved. This book or any portion thereof may not be reproduced or used in any manner whatsoever without the express written permission of the publisher except for the use of brief quotations in a book review.

Scriptures marked **KJV** are taken from the KING JAMES VERSION (KJV): KING JAMES VERSION, public domain.

NKJV Scripture taken from the New King James Version®. Copyright © 1982 by Thomas Nelson. Used by permission.

Scriptures marked **NLT** are taken from the HOLY BIBLE, NEW LIVING TRANSLATION (NLT): Scriptures taken from the HOLY BIBLE, NEW LIVING TRANSLATION, Copyright©1996, 2004, 2007 by Tyndale House Foundation. Used by permission of Tyndale House Publishers, Inc., Carol Stream, Illinois 60188.
All rights reserved. Used by permission.
AMP are taken from the AMPLIFIED BIBLE (AMP): Scripture taken from

the AMPLIFIED® BIBLE, Copyright © 1954, 1958, 1962, 1964, 1965, 1987 by the Lockman

Foundation Used by Permission.

Printed in the United States of America First Printing, 2023

ISBN: 978-1-7338770-9-1

McCurry Ministries International Publishing Assisting

TABLE OF CONTENTS

Acknowledgment v

Special Dedication vi

Introduction 1

Chapter 1: A Prophet in My Mother Womb 11

Chapter 2: Years of Abuse 15

Chapter 3: In Search of Love 21

Chapter 4: My Crack Addiction and Street Life 27

Chapter 5: The call of God 33

Chapter 6: God still calling 41

Chapter 7: All in God's plan 49

Chapter 8: Turning Back 63

    The Interlude: "It was his Blood" 69

Chapter 9: A Call to Himself 71

Chapter 10: My Hundred-Day Threshing Floor Experience .. 91

A passage: The sweet invite 113

The Scroll: Today's Church 117

Chapter 11: In the promise now 121

Chapter 12: The New Birth/ New beginning 127

About The Author let love sleep until time says it ready to be awakened.

.... 135

Acknowledgment

I acknowledge my Lord and Savior Jesus Christ who is first in my life; I give him all the glory for bringing me this far because he thought I was worth saving. I thank you, Lord, for counting me worthy to write, inspire, and be a prophetic voice to the nations in this hour. I will forever give you the glory and honor for your divine leading and inspiration of love and grace in this season. You will always be first and foremost in my life. It's because of you I'm still alive.

To my birth mother and father Alma D Blue and Sante Holton who birthed me into this world, you would be so proud of me mom of what I have become.

Special Dedication

To my mother, Alma D Wheeler who I know was a great woman who raised me until she wasn't able. I'm glad I still have some vivid memories of you. I wish you were still here mom.

To my three beautiful children Mario, Danielle, and De'shon Blue, whom I'm so proud of, and to my eight grandchildren and God children Joshua, Milesa, Tykisha and Alex

In remembrance of my Brothers and sister Malcolm and Mark Blue and Sister Debbie Blue.

To my oldest sister Regina Miller who has been a rock to our family and truly a blessing. To my other sister Vanetta for all your emotional support, Karen my baby sister I love you and Diana Blue you are appreciated. To my other brothers, Dennis Blue, who has been there for me over the years. Melvin jr. and Christopher Blue I truly love you.

To my true friends Vanessa Beckett, Debbie Werth, who has always prayed for me Sister Ruth and Pastor Derrick Waltz, and Priscilla Timberlake who have sowed into my life in a time of need and have been my friends for years. I can't thank you enough and to all of the people who have been there for me and who have sowed monetary gifts to me especially in a time of need. I give thanks to Deacon Ian Birks and his wife Elder

Richanda Birks and Special thanks Apostle McCurry and Pastor T McCurry for all of your encouragement and Prophet Jackson who spoke greatness into my life. My sister Prophetess Vivian Lions and Mama Brown you will never be forgotten.

To my Spiritual father in Christ Bishop C.I. Bordley who took me under your wing and taught me much wisdom and loved me unconditionally. I will never forget what you instilled in me. I still have a reservoir of Wisdom to this day. I love you dearly and miss you preaching and teaching the unadulterated word of God. I miss you so much.

To my Spiritual brother Ronald Bordley and his wife Debra Bordley, I love you dearly. I will never forget what you guys did for me over the years. To my brother from another mother Tabu Thank God for you and proud of what God has birthed out of you.

A Prophet's Memoir

Written by

Prophetess
Sandra Kaye Blue

A prophet in my mother womb

"Before I formed you in the womb I knew you; Before you were born sanctified you; I ordained you a prophet to the nations."

Jeremiah 1:5 - NKJV

Introduction

"For we are his workmanship, created in Christ Jesus for good works, which God prepared beforehand, that we should walk in them" **Ephesians 2:10 - NKJV**

A Prophet's Memoir is a narrative that highlights how God's purpose and calling in us are preserved even when the journey becomes hard, and the enemy plans to destroy us.

The scriptures say he will use the foolish things of the world to confound the wise 1 Corinthians 1:27.

To my dearest audience, my earnest desire is that you might be inspired by my story and be encouraged. To anyone who has been called with a gift but especially to the Prophets who are graced to carry the mantle and walk in the office of the Prophetic because of how important it is to be the mouthpiece for God. I do not take this mantle lightly.

The Lord told me to write this memoir in 2021, this was birthed out of my intimacy with God in prayer. It reflects the last twenty years of my life, from moving back home and walking through some of my hardest challenges in my life and walking out my purpose. All praises go to God, because not only did he recreate me, but help give birth to what he had ordained me to do from the foundation of the world. It all came through praying and seeking God's face, and believing in the process he took me through to get here.

Over the years from my experience and observation I've seen quite a bit in the ministry of our Lord and Savior Jesus Christ. I'm not here to judge, but to shed some light on what has become a stumbling block in the body of Christ for years mainly through vain traditions.

I believe the body of Christ has done the people of God a disservice not all, I must say but quite a bit, but the majority have spent too much time telling the born-again believers who they are not. Instead of who they are.

In my opinion, leaders whom God has ordained to oversee the church which is the body of Christ should, have enough discernment like the Apostle Paul. To see first what the gift and calling a person has and to impart, cultivate, and equip him or her for the betterment of the kingdom of God rather than hold them hostage to a pew. I've seen gifted people spend years in ministries not once given the opportunity to use their potential or talents. As a result, they never get to fulfill their God-given purpose. This is a travesty. Be that as it may, I am confident God is raising a favored generation who is willing to serve in the capacity to do what he or she has been called to do.

I understand in times past we had to go through the protocol for years waiting for someone to say when you're ready to move forward, of course in God's time. But now it's time to prepare, we are in another dispensation, and time is moving rapidly. One thing is for sure God will make sure you're on schedule if he must do it himself or send you somewhere where you can be properly trained so God's purpose can be fulfilled in you.

I'm not saying take any scripture out of context, the word of God says, make your calling and election sure. 2 Peter 1:10 and obey those who have the rule who watch for your soul Hebrews 13:17. "For he will finish the work and cut it short in righteousness because a short work will the Lord make upon the earth." Romans 9:28.

I'm talking about kingdom work, not church work. Everyone is not ordained to sit in the sanctuary and serve, some are called out of the four walls. If everyone is sitting in church how do we reach the world?

I'm not saying you've been saved two months and now you want to go start a church no that's not what i'm saying at all. I'm simply saying let's equip the people of God.

We are not there to build the leader's vision but to fulfill what God has called us to, we are there to follow them as they follow

Christ, obey them and they are there to lead us, feed us and to get us to full maturity through the taught or preached word of God. They are our under shepard. God told Peter to feed my sheep. John 21-15-17.

Here is a good scenario: just give this a thought for a few minutes. Most parents when they see their child take interest in something. For instance, he or she bangs on that old piano that has been sitting in the corner for years. And every day she or he goes and tries to play it, and it happens continually in your mind you say when they're older depending on their age you will start giving them piano lessons right? You acted on what you picked from your observation and they became the next Mozart.

So, it is in the spirit. When a church leader recognizes a calling in God's people when the time is right or by the leading of the Holy Spirit, I consider it the leader's responsibility to encourage such a gift or calling for the benefit of the Kingdom of God. That is why the body of Christ suffers from so many identity issues today and that's why The Spirit of jealousy and competition runs rampant in the house of God.. The church has become dysfunctional with no power. We have replaced the Spirit of God and the love of God with rules and religion. I don't know when the last time I felt a real move of God because nobody is willing to die. It is the anointing that destroys the yolk. I mean the real presence and power of God. I remember we would be in the service of the lord and the power of God would come down and sweep through the place and we would feel the residue of that service weeks later. The real presence and power.

Isn't it reassuring to tell someone what you see them becoming? It may build their self-esteem, help them to set goals and do something different in life. Have you ever been told by anyone you will never amount to anything? You will never be anything or, you're just like your no good father or mother. Literally, they kill someone's self-esteem, and sometimes it's the closest person to you, and sometimes they never get past their words. And we come into the church and get the same treatment God forbid. I have experienced so much in the body of Christ and you believe what is said because they are your Pastors, Apostles, and Prophets in the church not by the spirit but through the flesh. Let's stop killing the body the Lord will separate the goats from the sheep in that day.

Let's build up the men and women of God. Remember in the bible God had recognized Cornelius and needed Simon Peter to visit him. But, Simon Peter wouldn't go because he was condemnatory. He couldn't see the big picture and instead called what God had sanctified unclean because of stereotypes. In summary, God admonishes Simon Peter "What God has cleansed you must not call common" Acts 10:1-23. I've seen so much!

Furthermore, there are a lot of brave and unique talents hiding under the oak tree like Gideon Judges 6:11-14.or like when God sent Samuel to Jesse house to anoint David to be king.

It's a king in all of us.

Leaders are required in our dispensation by the grace of God to help birth out the next generations of Pastors, Evangelists, Prophets and Apostles so they can subdue kingdoms, take over territories and snatch people out of darkness. I'm not referring to your title but walking in purpose and walking in power behind that title which requires the work and service behind it. The difference was back then the Prophets, Apostles walked in signs, wonders, and miracles not for boasting but in demonstration of power for the glory of God.

Don't get me wrong everyone is not a pastor or prophet or teacher but we all are here to serve, however whatever it is let your gift or calling be used for the upbuilding of God's kingdom and to tearing down of satan. Let's learn how to serve. The scriptures say " Yet it shall not be so among you: but whosoever desires to become great among you shall be your servant.

There are so many gifted people in the house of God ready to move on purpose. I don't want this to sound contradictory but I want to make a point here. Let's not get the gift mixed up with the call. Gift and calling comes without repentance. The gift will get you there, the call will keep you there. I mean being equipped in character and walking in power that we may be a light to the world. I would rather be anointed with character opposed to having a gift with no character. A prophet with a gift that has not been purified is very dangerous.

Until Stephen and Philips were discovered, due to church disputes Acts 6:1-6 they were in the church like most of us today. Consider Timothy one of the early Bishops in the New Testament; it took the Apostle to discover, anoint, and inspire him to develop his gifts 1 Timothy 4:11-1

As you read this memoir you will discover God nudging you. He created us all for his purpose; there is a purpose in all of us. I encourage you to get into God's divine presence in prayer and ask God what is your purpose and what capacity he needs you to serve. I'm so glad God birthed me out the way he did by his own hands and power.

It wasn't always a pleasant experience but neither is having a natural baby, it comes with some pain and suffering for a minute. But when it's all said and done you birthed that little beautiful boy or girl. So it is in the spirit when God is birthing something out in you, you feel all the labor pains and the discomfort, just know it is for his will and purpose because you never know what you are giving birth 2 I think we forget there is a process to the madness. You must be tried and proven for the work, however nobody wants to go through the process.

A prophet's memoir was compiled with the help of the Holy Ghost who inspired me to narrate and take you through my journey, my life experiences, and my ups and downs and some painful trials I thought I would never walk out of. It is your partner as you come to terms with who you really are in God. I hope this memoir in your hand will enlighten your awareness, illuminate your mind, heal your pain, restore your identity, and stimulate you to press on. Knowing that whatever you've been through in your past does not dictate your future, recognizing that God has the power to restore anything that was destroyed or stolen. The majority doesn't know who they are, they live the way people dictate or the way society dictates. God's only desire is to live Vicariously through his people who he purchased with his own blood. Let's just put away all the religious antics and politics in ministry so people can get to their divine purpose in God and maybe just maybe we can be like Paul and turn the world upside down too.

As you get acquainted with the pages of A Prophet's Memoir you will begin to realize that Satan is always after those with the call of God on them and have a unique message for the world. Let's just say, before the world hated you, Satan already did and orchestrated the events in your life to derail the purpose of God for your life.

Do you have a calling or are you chosen? Do you have a dream or a unique destiny? Know Satan the enemy will come after you even as a newborn, such as when Moses was born or when Herod wanted to kill Jesus. God used Moses to deliver a whole nation and used Jesus to die for the whole world. They had what you call a FIRST anointing the first to ever do it. You wonder why you are going through so much hell, maybe you have a first anointing to. I know I do according to what God revealed to me. I think I might have to coin that phrase.

Finally, A Prophet Memoir is my testimony, a miracle in your hand with God's divine inspiration and power to transform your world. As you take your first step on this journey to explore the wonderful content of this memoir. "The Lord God Almighty shall arise and have mercy upon you: for the time to favor you, the set time is come" Psalms 102:13.

It is your season, get hold of it and push to your purpose...

Chapter 1

A Prophet in My Mother Womb

I was born to the late Santee Holton and Alma D. Wheeler on October 29, 1963. I grew up on the west side of Cleveland. At the age of six, I lost my mother to breast cancer. The only thing I remember was her lying in that hospital bed not feeling well. I did not understand what was going on at the time. I just knew something was wrong with my mother and everyone was gathered around her bedside.

Not long after my mother passed away in 1969. I was told my cousin promised to take care of me and my sister since we were the youngest of the siblings. I was six and my baby sister was about two years old. My cousin took care of us for a while but my baby sister ended up in a foster home some time later.

Looking at my childhood I cannot recollect any good memories. It was rough growing up. All I can remember is when

I first experienced real-life trauma as a kid.

It had to be when I was about 5 years old or younger, I remember using the bathroom when my youngest brother walked in and touched me between my legs inappropriately. I do not know where my mom was at the time. I was young but I will never forget it. It was embedded in my memory forever. Then, when I was about twelve years old, I was molested by my cousin's husband.

I am glad my baby sister went to foster care; otherwise, she would have been a victim of the same abuse as well.

We had all gone through some things in life; the untimely death of our mother affected my baby sister and me the most being the youngest in the family. I cannot chronologically remember my childhood experiences only events here and there but the trauma for sure because it was so real. All I know is that I felt so misplaced even as a kid in school. I had to be in first grade or second grade; my teachers really didn't know what ethnic background to associate me with. I could have passed for a biracial kid when I was younger because I was light-skinned, with green eyes, and long wavy hair.

Growing up without a mother was hard and not having a father present was even harder. It was only when I turned twelve years old that I met my biological father.

I just so happen to be going to the same junior high school as my half-sister. I was going to the study hall with some of my peers passing between classes, and we were having a conversation about our fathers. As we kept conversing, I mentioned my father's name because that's all I knew and if he came around, I certainly didn't remember. My sister looked at me with a very strange look and said aloud that's my father's name, of course, she went home and told her mother.

It was only then my father started picking me up on weekends, and I was able to meet the rest of my siblings. They stared at me and examined me up and down. I felt like a looked at a specimen, and it made me very uncomfortable. I was only twelve years old, and they considered me an outcast. Santee and I never really became close. Twelve years had passed. I was his well-kept secret until it was all exposed that day. I never held it against him, I barely knew the man except by the scent of his cigars. For me, all I knew the visits got shorter and shorter and as time went on eventually, they stopped altogether.

I believe the revelation that I was Santee's daughter started affecting my stepmother. I reminded her of his affair with my mother. She tried to put up a good front, but it didn't last, and she never got over it. They could not deny me if they wanted to, I looked just like their side of the family. It didn't matter. I felt so misplaced from both sides of my family again I didn't know where I fit in.

When I returned home to Cleveland in 2000, I was able to spend some time with my father before he passed away. I led him to the Lord right in the nursing home one afternoon. He was glad to see me, and he still had his right mind even at the age of ninety. It went well; I paid my respects when he finally passed in 2019. I sat at the back of the church. They never really claimed me anyway, besides my name was not going to be mentioned in the obituary, and they made that noticeably clear, cruel huh? I thought so. I was a reproach to their family. That's how they kept it. You see, I was rejected even from the beginning of time.

Chapter 2

YEARS OF ABUSE

I had no example of a father or a mother growing up and never knew what love really was. I honored my father, but I never had a relationship with him. My life was so unstable again I felt so misplaced.

All I knew was that I was a traumatized little girl from an immature age, and it followed me into my teenage years and adulthood. The evidence was obviously glaring to prove it, but nobody paid any attention, and I never found the solution to the pain until later when I gave my life to Christ. That's when the process of healing started. Traumas are so real on so many levels people should never make light of someone else's ordeal. You know how people say get over let it go until you walk in someone else's shoes just pray! That was just the beginning, it didn't stop there. Statistics say 93% of children who are abused in this country know their abuser.

What really affected me were the horrible things that I had to endure under my cousin's roof, the years of molestation. There were times when things really got so bad and unbearable for me. I lived with my two other cousins, but we never had a good relationship except for me and my boy cousin. I didn't know why my girl cousin never liked me. She was my first cousin's oldest daughter, so that made her my second cousin. Her grandmother and my mother were sisters. We fought every day, and it was her stepfather that molested me. Besides, she was very promiscuous herself, things I had seen, like her boyfriend sneaking over in the middle of the night when her parents weren't home. We knew exactly what they were doing. I did not feel close to anyone to confide in, not even my sisters. I told my cousin, but she didn't believe me. I just buried the pain and dealt with it the best way I could. Some days were better than others. I had so many mixed emotions and was so confused. I was always incredibly quiet in my teenage years then my behavior started changing drastically. I really became an introvert for years.

I Became Dysfunctional

I started getting into trouble during my junior high school days; I started smoking cigarettes and tried weed too. I guess it was my way of coping with the pain that I could never talk to anyone even until this day. My body would cringe when he came home drunk and often beat my cousin so badly. The torment and fear that gripped our lives because of the abuse were harrowing. We would be awakened out of our sleep by them fighting and someone would have to call the police. She would wake up the next morning with black eyes, busted lips, and bruises, and go through the same thing every time he came home drunk. It was a lot to witness being young and having to ingest that behavior day in and day out. You couldn't imagine the trauma we all suffered.

We were all scared he never hit us, but he beat the life out of her. There were times I wanted to run away, I think I did once and got into trouble when I came back. I didn't really care, it was my escape even if it was for a minute or an hour, and it was my relief. He was an alcoholic for years, and he ended up dying years later I knew I had to forgive him even if he never admitted what he had done to me, she never admitted anything either, but it never excused the fact I was a child she never protected me, then again how could she, she was a victim of abuse herself. I hated him and dealt with the abuse and shame. When I visited my sister on my mother's side, I never wanted to return home and nobody investigated the situation, they just knew I was unhappy.

There were times I truly felt sorry for her and other times I was glad she got what she deserved. By this time, she had two other children by him. I never really had time to be a normal teenager, but the situation made me grow up fast. I just wanted to be a normal kid, but circumstances took that from me and cost me my innocence.

Another World

I do not know what happened to me, to have left and gone to live with my oldest brother in Fort Wayne, Ind. maybe this was her way of saving me I'm not sure, but the damage was already done. I was fifteen, almost sixteen. I didn't grow up with him, and I didn't know what to expect, but anything was better than being there. It was extremely hard leaving my little cousins behind because of the attachment I did everything for them, I always had to babysit while everyone else was outside having fun, but it was good to finally be free. I lived there for a year and then from there, I moved to Dover, De. In 1979 with my other brother who was married and serving in the Military at the time, God had a plan for my life even if I didn't see it then, after settling in De. I was going on seventeen by then.

My brother enrolled me in school right away. I played sports and met new friends. I graduated late due to moving around and missing a lot of schooling. but I finished. I had three beautiful kids. The first one I had was at the age of twenty. Dover was a small town and a lot of military people retired there. I was from the city, so this was a change of pace for me, it's what I needed at the time. I had seen so much in the city growing up, the pimps, the prostitutes, and drugs, you name it, but it was not out in the open as it was in the latter years. We would witness the prostitute on the corners when we would ride downtown on special occasions.

They were behind or should I say a little slow in everything, music, the latest fashions, the latest dances, and what have you. City life was fast-paced, and this was country living all the way. I had never seen cows and farm animals before except when visiting a place called Cadiz, Ohio when we were little. I believe that's where my mother and grandmother grew up until my mother moved to Cleveland.

My brother was a strict military man. We were blood-related, but we didn't have a close relationship as sister and brother either. The only thing I remember is when I was little living with all of my siblings on the west side of Cleveland in a three-bedroom apartment way before my mother passed away or me visiting him when he was married to his very first wife. My oldest brother and sister were away at college, I guess. I'm not sure why we all didn't stay together after my mother died. No, one told me what really happened, but they never treated me any differently. We were all family; besides we all had the same blood running through our veins. Just different fathers, again, it affected me and my youngest sister the most. I still felt like an outcast. I can't imagine the trauma my little sister suffered also.

This was my brother's second wife, and she had three kids of her own. My brother only had one biological son Marcus. Raising my kids was challenging enough, but I had plenty of support, and I was thankful for it all. I knew nothing about being a mother since I really didn't have any examples growing up except taking care of my little cousins, I felt like I got the short end of the stick for years because of how I grew up.

Chapter 3

IN SEARCH OF LOVE

I had so many questions that were unanswered and nobody ever volunteered any answers. Why did my mother have to die? I had questions because I yearned for her love. It bothered me for years, something I knew I would never get to experience ever. My brother Mark really stepped up in such a critical time in my life, I am glad I got to thank him before he passed away.

However, it was a repeated cycle my kids knew their fathers except for my oldest, but them being a part of their lives they were absent because one was a married man with a family, my youngest son's father went to prison for murder, and one I hid for years because of the shame and embarrassment getting pregnant a second time. It was a messed-up situation all the way around. I was just in my twenties; It was family with my second child, but only through marriage.

I just wanted acceptance. I was young at the time confused, lost, and traumatized with no direction. I dealt with identity issues for years and low self-esteem even at that age, because of being molested by my brother and then by my cousin's abusive husband. I really wanted to seek other alternative measures at the time, but God had a bigger purpose for my life.

Trauma affects you mentally, emotionally, and physically. I was in an arrested development state of mind for years, not realizing this trauma was passed down through my bloodline, generational curses I was stuck in a time frame of my past. I was so undeveloped in so many areas of my life. I had to heal mentally and emotionally. It affected my state of being for years. I had to learn how to swim out of my stuck place. It wasn't until a friend of mine ministered to me on the phone one night that's when I realized where I was. I was trapped in my past, something started breaking that night, but this was years later. I was healed from my past but not from the trauma.

Having my second child we weren't blood-related, so, it wasn't incest, he took advantage of my inability to say no, and in my weakness, I allowed it to happen, and nobody knew until years later, I had one child already and another one on the way. I remember him reaching out to me exactly two weeks before he passed away. He called me back

In 2020, we talked a lot. His heart was heavy, and I could hear the sadness in his voice, and he was crying out for help. I believe at the time he was committed to the Muslim faith or just following the crowd. I really wanted to bring up some things from the past. I don't even think he was even aware of all those years, but I just held my peace. A lot of ill feelings started to come to the surface. He was young, and I was young, but I recognized that his heart was heavy, and with the cry that came from his soul all I could do was minister to him about giving his life to the one and only God. I'm thankful I was a listening ear. God is so merciful His hands are still stretched out toward us because of his love.

"The Lord is not slack concerning His promise, as some count slackness, but is longsuffering toward us, not willing that any should perish but that all should come to repentance." (2 Peter 3:9)

I began to pray for him, and the compassion and the love of God kicked in. He shared a lot with me and all he wanted was his mother's love.

Knowing what I know now we had the same battle, although I didn't grow up with either of my parents. Perhaps, that is why he drank so much or stayed in trouble to get her undivided attention. Although his mother was present I knew her, she was a good woman. She was married to my brother, but I don't know what transpired years later or what happened to their relationship. I never detected any disconnect.

When you grow up with both parents in the home it's truly a

blessing and something to be thankful for. I didn't have either.

I believe it was the following week he passed away. I'm so glad he got a chance to know and spend time with his daughter over the years.

A Thankful Heart

One thing God had to teach me was you can't give what you never received. That's just a fact. You can't become what you never had or experienced.

You can't be a good father or mother if you never had any example of any or don't know what that looks like. I had some jacked-up relationships with men, but the best one so far was my relationship with Christ. He was my example.

I am so glad my brother gave my kids that father figure presence they needed growing up because of his strict military background and he was a man. I thank God for my sons. They are the greatest fathers to their children and my daughter is a great mother to hers. My parents' lifestyle affected me, and my life affected theirs and the cycle continued. I know it hurt my kids in some ways even if they never talked about it, but it will be their story to tell one day. I'm not proud of my past but I know God has my future. I can remember dedicating them back to God even when they were little children and raised them in church in my earlier years.

I can't change my past and I truly had to learn to forgive

myself over the years. All I can do is thank God for where he has brought me from.

My kids are everything to me, and I am so proud of them despite their upbringing, they surprisingly turned out to be great children.

Dealing With the Enemy Within

I had buried trauma for years; I mean years I was saved but not healed. The funny thing is sometimes you don't realize it's the buried trauma that has not been dealt with. It's like you're in a grave separated from Light. Can you imagine all the unhealed people in the world that have suffered trauma in their life.

There were still a lot of challenges for me, it went from bad to worse, I mean it got worse, and life continued to take its course trying to raise two kids, things got hard. There were times I didn't know what was going to happen. I knew I had to raise my kids the best way I could and getting strung out on drugs made things so much more complicated. It was one of the biggest mistakes of my life. This is how it all started....

Chapter 4

MY CRACK ADDICTION AND STREET LIFE

I met a guy who had just got out of prison doing five years for selling drugs to an undercover cop. I never had any meaningful relationship. It was sex and that was it, but this guy was different, or so I thought. I had no idea what real love was. All that I had been through anyone I thought showed me any affection was mistaken for love, especially from the opposite sex. I had a narrow mind I believe came from the undelivered trauma I suffered growing up. We dated for seven years. He treated me well for the most part. We called ourselves in love; we lived together until he went back to prison. We both worked and did the best we could until we both got strung out on drugs.

The Unforgettable Night

I had many regrets but this one by far was the biggest I

remember. It is like it was yesterday, a night I will never forget when I took that first hit.

It was about the mid-80s when the crack era hit. It was prevalent in black neighborhoods and our communities. We became a product of our own environment. It was a war on drugs at one point all over the world. There was a party one night, and my boyfriend asked me to come with him. I was not the partying type, I really enjoyed my time at home, and I was more like a homebody.

He had convinced me to go, so we got dressed. We always complimented each other whenever we went out; he was tall, dark, and handsome. That's the type of man I was attracted to. I was not shabby myself. I had long pretty hair, a shape to die for, was light-skinned, and had the nickname redbone. When we arrived at his friend's house the party was already packed that night. We danced and mingled for a while. It started getting late and people were leaving, but we were invited to stay. We were escorted to a back room with just a few of us, we sat down, and his friend brought out a tray full of white stuff.

I was so paranoid I thought the police would bust in any minute, the music was already loud and if they did, we all were going to jail. I remember his friend gave my boyfriend a box of baking soda and a cup of water and asked him to cook it up. I sat back and saw the entire process.

I had heard of this stuff but had never actually seen it up close and personal until that night. He poured the white powder into the tube, mixed some baking soda with it, then added water, and lit the bottom with a lighter. What was a powdered form turned into a solid white rock. This was the first time I saw how cocaine was cooked up and became crack.

When he finished cooking the cocaine, he poured it out on the table, crumbled the big white rock with his hands, broke it into little pieces, and it was up for grabs like bees on honey. I could not understand what all the hype was about. I smoked weed before, but I never liked the way it made me feel so I stopped. Why was everybody so anxious over this white stuff?

I remember my boyfriend put a piece of the crack in his pipe along with some others and then he lit that pipe and inhaled, then exhaled, he could not speak for at least ten minutes exactly it left him speechless. I nudged him. I was scared at this point, but his friend assured me he was okay. He just had a rush. Everybody was so focused on getting high, I just watched. It was one of the best products on the market called fish scale, some of the best cocaine you could buy.

I was a little pissed because he was indulging the whole time. This was not his first rodeo from what I saw. I knew he sold it but smoking it, I was clueless until that night. This was the first time I had seen how crack really affected people; it was plentiful all over you could get it at a drop of a dime.

They begged me to try it. I refused, then after a while, I gave in. That's when they walked me through the process one step at a time.

First, they gave me the pipe. Secondly, they put a piece of the crack in it and told me to inhale while they lit the pipe, then I exhaled.

I tell you that was the best feeling I had ever experienced. It was a rush out of this world. My heart started beating fast and I couldn't even speak. That was the beginning of my seven-year drug addiction when I took that first hit, something I swore I would never do. Hitting it for the first time was too much, but it soon became my reality. I started chasing the ghost from that night on, people often asked what is, "chasing the ghost?" It is when you chase that first rush you felt when you tried it for the first time. You want that same experience repeatedly; it makes you feel like you could conquer anything. It would make you steal from your own mamma to get your hands on some of it.

You would be out there for days in the streets not knowing you have not been to work on the job you have had for the last ten years in two weeks because you lost track of time seriously. It makes you forget about everything and everybody who is important in your life. Can you believe that? I've seen the imaginable being in the streets, something I wouldn't want to ever experience again in life.

The Ghetto Chemist and the Drug Dealer

This drug addiction had no preference; black, white, young, or old were involved. I became a ghetto chemist. I cooked vast quantities and went into business for myself later down the road when my boyfriend went back to prison. This was his second time and seeing how much money could be made because everybody was hooked, I watched and gambled on my future. I always had the desire to become somebody great, yet I became a drug dealer hustling in the streets day and night. I was dealing with clients who were business people, lawyers, you name it, people in high places, everybody was either sniffing, shooting up, or freebasing cocaine back in the day.

I had gained such a rapport with my customers they kept coming back because I had some of the best dope and nobody messed with me because they knew who I was connected to. The strip was where we sold our drugs, a place where everybody hung out and gambled, sat in the bar, drank, and did their thing, or behind closed doors which was safe opposed to being out in the open.

It was like a mini-Vegas strip with a lot of dope coming in and out of the city and like I said it was plentiful. I worked for a kingpin drug dealer at first, who dealt with the big weight. For some reason, they liked me and from there it was on and popping. Being an incredibly good-looking woman back then didn't hurt at all either. I was just getting started learning the business and they trusted me.

My boyfriend was out selling one night and ended up getting in trouble and going back to prison for five more years. As I mentioned earlier I met him coming out of prison after doing a five-year bit, and was with him when he went back. We always hustled together besides; he was the one that introduced me to crack in the first place.

THE CALL OF GOD

"For many are called are chosen but few are chosen"
-Mathew 22:14

A couple of weeks before that happened, we were getting high one night because we decided we were going to chill that night. I had sold out of the dope I had, and it was late, so he went on the block to grab some more dope from somebody else. You had to be careful because you could get anything that time of night. I remember after he left, I was sitting in my living room and heard someone calling my name. I thought I was losing my mind or just simply high off the crack. I heard Sandra three times; it was a voice I had never heard. I heard it, then again, then a third time. He called me like he did Samuel in the Bible (1 Samuel 3:1-10). I swear....

It was a voice like no other. It broke through my high

intellect and every part of my being I heard it audibly. I didn't know it then, but it was the voice of God calling me the whole time, a voice I will never forget, it was time to come in. I had lost everything including my kids. I ended up giving my brother temporary custody of my children. I knew I had to survive, I had nobody, and my family didn't want to be bothered, they just talked about me, it was easier for them to talk about me then to get me some help.

After my boyfriend went back to prison the second time, I was still out there in the streets selling dope and smoking at the same time just trying to survive. I knew I had to be careful, because it was getting dangerous, and the feds had raided one of our key suppliers' homes, and he ended up doing forty-five years in prison.

The devil wanted to destroy my life as a child and didn't have any plans on stopping until I was dead. I was bound and didn't have the power to stop. Anyone, saying they never enjoyed sin would be telling a lie because I loved what I was doing until God started tugging on my heart. I was lost with no direction.

Though I loved the street life, I didn't belong there. I simply got caught up in the game, and it cost me almost everything almost my life. I went from selling so much dope and making money to just getting high every day to support my thousands-dollar a day habit. I had lost complete control of what was fun starting out just as a weekend thing, in the beginning, now it became my everyday lifestyle. I went to sleep hitting the pipe and would wake up the next morning doing the same thing to get my day started. My addiction would have me chasing that feeling back into the next night, and repeating the same cycle the next day, and the day after. I was a crack feen for real.

The Crack Drudge

Things had begun to change drastically, being out in the streets for that long I learned how to cook it, and what type of cut to put on it. I learned how to weigh it and then get it ready for distribution. I knew what was good, what was bad, what was pure, and what was not so pure. I enjoyed what I was doing for the most part. I just liked being part of the family, and they treated me like their sister, but I was tired of being out there, I didn't eat for days because it simply took my appetite away, and I was losing weight like crazy. I didn't look like myself anymore; I was going down fast after years of freebasing crack cocaine. I carried my tools everywhere I went so I wouldn't have to get someone else high because I didn't have my own tools. I was like an alcoholic with his liquor bottle.

I was in the streets for seven years, and I made a lot of money and smoked a lot of dope because I was my best customer. I lost my job, self-respect, and the place we were living in at the time, so I was homeless sleeping in the streets. I didn't bathe for days at a time, let alone change my clothes. I was a crack addict and spent days and hours in crack houses getting high. Despite what was going on, God was tugging on my heart even more. I just didn't have the will and strength to fight.

> *For when we were still without strength, in due time Christ died for the ungodly. 7 For scarcely a righteous man will one die; yet perhaps for a good man someone would even dare to die. 8 But God demonstrates His own love toward us, in that while we were still sinners, Christ died for us.* **(Romans 5:6-8)**

The twilight

After a while I started thinking about my kids heavily. I was doing the same thing day after day week after week, and year after year with no purpose just out there wasting my life away. It was times I wanted to commit suicide, I spent several days thinking about how I was going to pull it off, but I thought about my kids, being strung out had me wanting to end it all. The enemy had taken my mind, and he wanted my life. I remember hearing the devil's voice one night lying in bed. The enemy said to me, I'm coming for revenge I heard it, so clearly I jumped up and couldn't go back to sleep and my heart was beating fast. It was so audible.

I learned what I learned by being in the streets all those years. There were times I sat in our warehouse where we kept our supply bagging up so much dope. It was unheard of, that's the kind of dealers I worked for and the life I was living and they treated me like royalty. They were big-time, and I was a part of their operation. They taught me the game, and that's how I became a ghetto chemist. I cooked it up in big pots like your mama does when she is cooking a big pot of greens on the stove or something, or simply in tubes the ones the cigar came in. I learned to cut it and like I said, put it in some small capsules or baggies and sold it. I made money but eventually, it went right back into my pipe.(up in smoke)

We all dabbled, shoving it up our noses and hitting the pipe while we were dealing, I just lost control. One thing I began to realize is that I was strung out, and too many things were starting to happen to me. My friends were dying and going to prison.

Saved From Prison

Finally, I started paying attention. I thank God I never went to prison, but I had some close calls. It was a Friday night and one of my friends called me and asked me to take her to the city to get some drugs. I agreed. We drove to the city to pick up some dope, so she could flip and double her money, on our way back we got stopped by the police. I just knew we were going to jail. I was scared. My friend had just done time. I had never been to prison. I believe we had to pick up her son that same night. He was sitting in the police station with dope on him.

When the cop pulled us over, he asked for my driving license and registration. I'm glad I was always legit; he searched the car and found no drugs because we hid all that dope in a Pringle's can that was in my car under my seat, he never checked it. You are talking about being nervous. We drove back down the road so fast, if that cop had found the drugs that night, we would still be in prison today. I can't really remember how much it was, I just know it was a lot.

You are talking about God's mercy. We both laughed about it today but it wasn't anything funny that night. The judges were giving out a lot of time for drug trafficking. This is the same place where Harriett Tubman took the route from Dover to Wilmington to free the slaves. They still had a monument of a plantation there; it was still a racist state if you ask me. It was a historical place they called the small wonder. The First state where a lot of military people retired, my brother was stationed there for years before I came. He was there during the Jim Jones era when they brought the bodies to Dover Air Force base's because it was the largest US military mortuary.

We were playing on dangerous territory and the walls were closing in on me. I was strung out so bad I was unrecognizable to some and would be up for days at a time. I was pregnant with my third child who was conceived while I was in the streets on drugs and eventually, he ended up going into the court system. I was smoking during my pregnancy, it was God's mercy he didn't come out shaking, that's how bad I was strung out. God protected him even in my womb. I had no control, the crack had me bound. I was addicted to the way it made me feel, I went to another place when I got high it made me forget about everything at that present moment, except when I came down and reality kicked in. I just spent 1,000 in one complete hour sometimes in thirty minutes that's just how it was literally. This was a different drug from heroin, it got expensive. When I ran out of money, I knew how to hustle to buy more.

Chapter 6

GOD STILL CALLING

My intuition was telling me it was time to give my life to Christ or something bad was going to happen to me. I remember one night we left Dover and went to Philadelphia, the worst part with some friends of mine to get some dope. Well, once we got up there, we ran right smack dead into a shootout and got stranded in a bad snowstorm. My so-called friends ended up leaving us up there stranded, dead in the middle of winter for two days straight.

I thought I was going to die that night, bullets flying everywhere. We jumped out of the car and ran for cover. I almost got busted going to pick up dope, was right in the midst of a shoot-out, and had a bounty on my head because my best friend Michael Rue robbed a drug dealer one night. Then, my friend Gale committed suicide by jumping in front of a moving train.

Most of my friends were dying one after the other. People were overdosing just as we were getting high in crack houses. It was getting scary, and I wanted out of the game for good. But, Satan held me in captivity.

I couldn't stop getting high. I couldn't control my addiction either; staring at death right in the face and witnessing a drug addict that needed to be resuscitated due to an overdose from shooting too much dope into his arm. You would have thought that was enough. I kept getting high right in the midst of it was too high to even assist him, sick stuff right? Thank God he didn't die.

I just got a kick out of seeing the pipe filled with a white cloud of smoke when I lit it and the effect it had on me once I inhaled and exhaled. My other friends enjoyed putting the needle in their arms, but, it wasn't for me, everybody had their preference. I was so addicted and couldn't stop. I hate to take my mind back to my past because of what I saw and experienced being in the streets all those years. My friends, dying of AIDS as a result of HIV infections from sharing needles and crack had us strung out bad. I didn't care how I had to get my next dose but I had boundaries I would hustle. I was addicted, it was so hard to stop, and it was everywhere. It was like a never-ending carnival. On several occasions, I wanted to quit but I had no strength in me or the will to do so. Little did I know then, that I was his slave. The scriptures teach; us you become a slave to whatever you submit yourself to. I was in prison without bail, but looking back I sometimes wonder how I got over it. The devil had me and I was obeying his every command.

> *16 Do you not know that to whom you present yourselves slaves to obey, you are that one's slaves whom you obey, whether of sin leading to death, or of obedience leading to righteousness?* **(Romans 6:16 NKJV)**

I remember getting paid on a Friday. My check would be about eight hundred dollars. I would get off work; go right to the crack house, sit and blow every dime once I started. I didn't care how I was going to eat or pay my bills; it didn't matter, in my mind I was confident I would find a way to get the money back. I was just desperate to get high. I wanted to experience that rush over and over again, that desire to get high took precedence over everything, even the will to live.. It never worked out that way though; because it's all in your mind being under Satan's control lying to you and manipulating your reasoning. Like I said, I got high because I was addicted to the way it made me feel, no one addicted to anything just wants to be addicted. It helped me deal with the hidden pain; it was my coping mechanism. I didn't have a care in the world until I came down and realized how much money went up in smoke. There goes the bill money and rent money, this happened in the earlier stages when I thought I was a functioning addict like a functioning alcoholic. I was lying to myself. I was sinking like quicksand. I couldn't pull myself out. - I would say okay this is it and be right back at it the next hour when somebody offered to get me high again.

Signs It Is Time to Quit

We had major connections but, in this game, anything could go wrong, anybody could turn you on just like in the movies. The dope game was real, and it was time for me to get out. As usual, I was helpless. By this time, I was strung out, it didn't matter if I sold it, and I was waist-deep in SIN. It was going right back into my system. I messed up plenty of people's dope. I didn't care who it belonged to or whether it was mine, theirs, or whoever I didn't care. If I wanted to get high I did just that. I would have to hide out for some days because I didn't know what they were going to do to me, smoking up their ounces of cocaine. I'm telling you it was the mercy of God nobody ever beat me up, or jumped me, they might have been hell mad, but that was it, they turned around and gave me more dope to sell because they knew what I was capable of but, eventually it stopped. I just felt it was fair game.

> *"If it had not been for the Lord who was on our side when men rose up against us, then they had swallowed*

us up quickly when their wrath was kindled against us."
(Psalms 124:1 NKJV)

I didn't care about anything. I felt like it was my right and things went left. I usually went and found my friend Michael when I knew I was going to smoke up a package and would be out of sight for three to four days. I mean I did this for 7 years slinging dope and smoking it hustling in the streets day in day out everyday. I mean smoking crack was my life. but God.

The turning point for me to go to detox was when my friend Michael spent all his money on drugs one night. Unfortunately, I wasn't with him that night. But, he came and got me and told me what happened. As a result, he decided to rob a notorious drug dealer at gunpoint. This fool put on a ski mask with a gun and went into the dope dealer's house because he spent all his money, and the dope dealers wouldn't front him for more drugs. You see, once you are hooked on drugs your mind is twisted, and some of the insane things are better imagined than experienced. Michael wasn't an exception. So, he made up this horrendous idea of robbing a cruel drug mogul. This heralded my first step toward quitting the game.

I believe that was my exit. If it wasn't for that, I would never have gone to rehabilitation. God used him to save and change my life that night. I believe it was the same night the cops raided the strip, and my friend Michael found the dope dealer's drugs hidden in the trees that night. I will never forget that night.

We sat behind his mother's house and smoked the drug dealer's dope that night, and the dope he found we poured it all out. It had to be about a hundred bags or more. We cooked it up, and smoked until the next morning, deciding what was going to be our next move. We were so high that morning. I don't even remember how we made it to the hospital. I didn't rob him, but I was guilty by association. Those boys were ruthless and had migrated from New York, D.C. People were getting killed and never found. They were gangsters; they didn't play about their money or drugs. People were crazy in the 80s. They were lacing embalming fluid in weed and smoking it; they called it "Wet" back then. Folks would be in the street butt naked acting a fool you hear me it was scary.. I mean I haven't told half of what I went through and experienced in the streets because time and space will not permit me. I've seen some stuff.... in my days. I'm just keeping it real things got real bad. At times, I thought I was going to die out there in the streets.

It was the next morning we decided enough was enough. Somehow we made it to the nearest hospital and told them we were addicted to crack. God used him that night because he knew whatever Michael did; I was going to follow, and the same with him. We got high, sold dope together, and were around each other every day. I mean we were inseparable, we were friends to the end and eventually, our friendship diminished over the years. I heard he was dying of Cancer.

What an incredible and merciful God, who understands and

loves us so much despite the bad things we have done, and horrible things we have experienced in this world . Just know that Jesus is our conquering king. He is such a forgiving God and loves us unconditionally and is willing to forgive.

> *37 Yet in all these things we are more than conquerors through Him who loved us. 38 For I am persuaded that neither death nor life, nor angels nor principalities nor powers, nor things present nor things to come, 39 nor height nor depth, nor any other created thing, shall be able to separate us from the love of God which is in Christ Jesus our Lord* **(Romans 8:37-39 NKJV)**.

The Lord was my stay.

Chapter 7

ALL IN GOD'S PLAN

11 For I know the plans I have for you," declares the Lord, "plans to prosper you and not to harm you, plans to give you hope and a future **Jeremiah 29:11 NIV**

After waiting in the hospital for hours that morning they sent us to a detox facility for seven days. It was one of the happiest weeks of my life. I was tired and scared. I wanted to stay longer but at that time no long-term beds were available. I was sick and tired of being sick and tired. I sold drugs and got high for years. The devil tried to destroy my life, but God snatched me from the pit of hell. My mind, body, and soul were tired. I was truly ready for a change. God in his mercy and endless love was calling me. (Matthew 11:28-30).

28 Come to Me, all you who labor and are heavy laden, and I will give you rest. 29 Take My yoke upon you and learn from Me, for I am gentle and lowly in heart, and you will find rest for your souls. 30 For My yoke is easy and My burden is light." (Matthew 11:28-30)

God Set Me Up

I stayed clean for ten years after that seven-day treatment. It just felt good not to have smoked crack for a whole week.it. For God's divine purpose, I ran into Pastor Bordley who was the pastor of Greater Love Temple and later became my pastor and father in the Lord. It was him and another lady everybody called Sister Barbara who used to witness to me about the Lord. When we saw her crossing the street the drug dealers and the crack addicts would literally run, like she was a Jehovah's Witness. You know how we do when they come knocking on the door we hide and pull the window shades down.

She truly was on an assignment from God. It seemed like when I tried to run, my feet became like brass. I was running, in my mind, but my body would not move. She caught me every time, and she would say to me Jesus loves you. It is time for you to give your life to Christ. I was truly miserable, and I knew she could discern that back then. I believe looking back now she must have been a prophet of God; she always stayed to herself, was a praying woman, and was very misunderstood. She made sure I was right there to listen. I knew she was right especially when I heard Jesus calling my name that night.

God Provided A Way

Once I got released my biggest fear was going back on the streets, but God had me in the right place at the right time. God placed me in the care of Bishop Bordley and Sister Barbara. I talked to him about my fears of going back in the streets and if I did I wasn't going to make it. The next day he told me to meet him at the address he gave me; he knocked on the door and introduced me to the lady who was overseeing the rooming house. To my amazement the woman Bishop Bordley introduced me to, was the same woman who had been witnessing to me all those years, Good old Sister Barbara God had me hook line, and sinker. If that wasn't a setup, I don't know what it was. The whole experience let me know that God loved me and wanted me to give my life to him because he knew what plans he had for me.

I ended up staying there until I was able to get up on my feet. Pastor Bordley had put me in safe hands. Sister Barbara watched me like a hawk and reported everything I did. He knew the process of my getting delivered was on the way. Once I got settled, I started attending church because it was mandatory to go at least once a week. When I found a job, I would let Sister Barbara hold my money until I got stronger because it was my trigger to use it again, and I didn't want to take any chances until I got stronger.

My friend Michael came around a lot, but there was no turning back for me. Bishop would tell me he's not ready, you're going to have to cut him off. He saw something I didn't, and he was right Michael never became fully committed to serving God. As I consider the thought of cutting him off, something was telling me to obey the man of God. Eventually, I separated from him. It was difficult though. It was hard to break off from Michael because we had soul ties. He was my best friend; nonetheless, my mind was made up, and the man of God was right.

In the rehabilitation center, there's a saying "to be successful you must change people, places, and things." I was sincere about getting my life back together. I lived in one room for months until I was able to do better. Boy, was I grateful? Anything was better than going back on the streets. I was truly tired of smoking crack every day and not being with my children was really affecting me badly.

After getting settled in that one room for months it felt great! It felt like I was in heaven, I had not slept in a good bed for years except when I booked a hotel room when I was out there selling drugs. But, for the most part, I was homeless. Having somewhere permanent to lay my head meant everything. I started going to church learning about God and being around some sanctified folks helped me tremendously. I had never felt this kind of love before it was real. I had spiritual mothers and a spiritual father. Something I was missing my whole life, everything felt so right.

A Changed Life

After attending church for a while one Sunday morning Bishop Bordley was preaching the word of God, he made an altar call, and I walked up there with tears running down my face, I was under conviction.

I gave my life to God in 1989. I weighed 90 pounds when I went to that altar that day. God saved me and baptized me. Later on, during Sunday School, Minister Poole laid hands on me, and I was filled with the Holy Ghost. I was excited about God and what he had done for me. I was eating well, and picked back up some weight. I thank God for Bishop Bordley, he took me and his nephew Tabu under his wing. Bishop Bordley had a special love for drug addicts because God had delivered him from Heroine. We were close and my father in the Lord taught me plenty..

He truly was a father I never had. He treated me like his daughter, and I respected him like a father. I miss him dearly, what he instilled in me will be with me for a lifetime. He taught me much wisdom and really exemplified the true love of God. He always told me to keep a good name no matter what. I try to live up to that in my everyday walk with God. My spiritual mothers showed me by example what Holiness looked like. Mother Macklin walked with so much grace and compassion. I can still hear her graceful voice and see that great big smile. She went on to be with the lord. I loved her dearly. I remember some of the talks we used to have.

On the other hand, Mother Carroll who is still living presently would tell you just like it was, they both had their unique way of doing things, and how they handled the women in the church, but they were Godly women. We had real church mothers back in the day; this was all new to me.

My spiritual father kept us in line. He was a very stern man, but he had such a balance and walked in much wisdom, and knew how to rebuke in love. He made me cry plenty of times, but it made me. The truth was I never had the discipline I needed growing up. It was good to know somebody was concerned about my well-being.

> *I loved him dearly. The Bible says when my father and my mother forsake me, Then the Lord will take care of me (Psalms 27:10). This was literally my testimony.*

I miss him so much - Bishop Bordley. He deposited so much into me over the years. As time went on, I became active in the ministry. I was a choir director, started learning how to become a musician, an usher worked with the youth, and had a deep love for God. I got my own place some years later and took my son back as well. By now my older children were teenagers, so I got visiting rights although my brother's third wife made it difficult because she had other motives. I guess they couldn't believe God had delivered me. I had to prove myself though, it was hard. My experience with my brother's family after my deliverance underscores Ananias's response to God when he asked him to meet Saul after he was converted on the way to Damascus. I had to be proven sometimes people don't believe you can be changed but I was living proof of what God had done.

> *10 Now there was a certain disciple at Damascus named Ananias; and to him the Lord said in a vision, "Ananias." And he said, "Here I am, Lord." 11 So the Lord said to him, "Arise and go to the street called Straight, and inquire at the house of Judas for one called Saul of Tarsus, for behold, he is praying. 12 And in a vision he has seen a man named Ananias coming in and putting his hand on him, so that he might receive his sight." 13 Then Ananias answered, "Lord, I have heard from many about this man, how much harm he has done to Your saints in Jerusalem. 14 And here he has authority from the chief priests to bind all who call on Your name." (Acts 9:10-14 NKJV).*

However, God reassured Ananias that Saul was a changed man.

> *15 But the Lord said to him, "Go, for he is a chosen vessel of Mine to bear My name before Gentiles, kings, and the children[c] of Israel. 16 For I will show him how many things he must suffer for My name's sake." (Acts 9:15-16 NKJV).*

I never killed anyone, but I was a drug addict and God changed my life, but the suffering I can certainly relate to.

I may not have been there for my kids during my drug abuse, I had raised them during the younger part of their life until I got strung out. I was their mother and nobody could ever change that.

With my youngest son, I had to go through a long court battle until they saw that I was a fit mother to care for him and again I had to be proven again and that was understandable.

God Arranged a Foster Parent for My Son

God had a Christian woman adopt him; it was all in God's plan. Things were working out, and God was putting my life back together, but it was a process. I remember asking God who was this woman who had adopted my son because back then once things were final you had no information, but, the only thing I knew was her first and last name. God was with me, and he knew my heart.

This Is Just One of My Testimonies

One morning I had to go and drop some things off at the cleaners. I always knew the ladies' name, but never knew who she was, and what she looked like. The Lord had ordered my steps that morning. I walked into the cleaners that day and the teller was talking with her and asked what her name was. She replied; Leona Baines from that day forward I was able to meet her and introduce myself, and we became good friends.

That was my son Nana. She treated us well and helped us so much. God had her adopt my son at the right time. She was a woman of God, and He used her for my son. Mrs. Baines used to tell me years ago it was something special about that little boy that caught her attention. It was all God. She went on to be with the Lord also. I was growing up in the ministry but still young in the Lord. I was enjoying what God was doing for me and things were looking up.

Like Saul I Became a Preacher of Jesus Christ

Like Saul after his conversion, I would go back to my same stomping ground and witness to people about God; it was undeniable what God had done for me. I had to tell them if God did it for me, he will do it for you. I gave the world hope through my testimony. I mean again "tore up from the floor up." I know it's an old cliché but it's the truth.

They knew me, when I was smoking crack, they couldn't deny that there was a God in heaven and he was real. After seeing me cleaned up and transformed I was their conviction. I had to preach Christ the true and living God. Some were amazed and heard how God transformed my life.

> *20 Immediately he preached the Christ in the synagogues, that He is the Son of God. 21 Then all who heard were amazed, and said, "Is this not he who*

*destroyed those who called on this name in Jerusalem, and has come here for that purpose, so that he might bring them bound to the chief priests?" 22 But Saul increased all the more in strength, and confounded the Jews who dwelt in Damascus, proving that this Jesus is the Christ **(Acts 9:20-22)**.*

Freedom at last

17 Now the Lord is the Spirit; and where the Spirit of the Lord is, there is liberty (2 Corinthians 3:17).

Let me include this Satan has been a liar from the beginning; he tricks us and deceives us about our life. He wants to keep us from our freedom and destroy our confidence; He creates false security hoping you never come into the knowledge of truth. knowing his time is short and in reality he wants to keep you for his kingdom but God purchased me for his.

I was enjoying life. It was simply good to be free and God was moving in my life. I had a love for God and his people. I was on fire for God. I wanted to save the entire world when God saved me. I had such a zeal for God.

The Proposal:

I was enjoying Jesus until a young man of God took an interest in me and wanted to marry me. I had to be saved for about two, maybe three years, and still a babe in Christ. We dated, but it didn't work out. He ended up marrying someone else from another church. He was my first love and first heartbreak in the church. I'm truly glad God blessed him. It was a learning experience and one of the hardest trials I went through being a babe in Christ. You know how it is when you first get saved you think everyone is saved.

He got married, and she ended up joining our ministry because that's what we were taught. That's what I had to face. Truly, it was an adjustment for all of us, but God brought me through. I learned some things through that experience and that was (Song of Solomon 8:4) that ye stir not up, no awake my love, until he please.

I was still growing in God in some areas, I still needed deliverance. Thank you, Bro Kevin Williams; you helped me get really delivered. This was just part of my journey. He was a great man of God with a good reputation who I genuinely cared for. It wasn't his entire fault I didn't think I was ready at the time God was still working on me, and things just happened incredibly fast. I have no regrets. It was truly an honor; besides, there were other women who were waiting to get married, but he chose me. (Proverbs 18:22) He that finds a wife finds a good thing.

However, I needed deliverance from my buried trauma which he knew nothing about, rejection, dad issues, fear, abandonment issues, and trust issues just to mention a few. I'm so glad I'm delivered today. I had no regrets. God used that situation to dig some things out of me, and it didn't feel pleasant, but it worked out for my good.

A church mother I met, used to say, "God will work out all of your fine details" boy, was she right? Sometimes, God will use the closest thing to you to make you. I'm glad God gave him a wife and two beautiful kids later. I'm just being transparent. I'm sharing my experiences and how I overcame some things. It wasn't easy, but it made me into the woman I am today. God has kept me for the last twenty-three years as a single woman, now I believe if I'm given the opportunity again, I have been processed out and would be a great gift to any man of God. And believe me; I'm not looking for whatever his will is for my life. I will be satisfied.

l love what Solomon wrote in the Scripture 8-4. I charge you, O daughter of Jerusalem, that ye stir not up, nor wake my love, until he please. Women must use wisdom dealing with the opposite sex because emotions not governed properly by the Holy ghost can be dangerous. What I'm trying to say is don't let anyone wake up love prematurely. True love is pure with all the right intentions, let love sleep until it pleases. Don't excite my feeling until I'm ready to experience real love because love is romantic and special and nothing to be played with let love wait too be awakened. When time is ready love will blossom like the roses on a summer day in a well-kept garden of true love. So, guard your heart and your precious rubies until love awakes it will be worth the wait. (Psalms 51-6) Behold, thou desire truth in the inward parts: and in the hidden part thou shalt make me to know wisdom.

I continued to work in the ministry while working on my relationship with my kids, building back what the enemy tried to destroy. God was keeping me as a single woman in the church, but surely there were some wolves in sheep's clothing waiting to devour our Godly women. One thing I can say is we had a Pastor who was truly a watchman on the wall.

Chapter 8

TURNING BACK

As a dog returns to his vomit, so a fool repeats his folly
Proverbs 26:11

I'm not sure what year it was when I moved to Atlanta, me and my son. I don't remember exactly why I left, probably needed to regroup a bit. We stayed with Mother Brown, who was a woman of God that I had developed a relationship with over the years. She truly was a blessing to me (Rip). Mamma Brown opened her home up to us. We lived there for about a year and after that year we returned home to Delaware and moved next door to my son's grandmother. By then I had about ten years of sobriety and ended up backsliding right in the house of God.

I had gotten really discouraged and ended up going right back out there on the street smoking crack. I didn't stay long this time, but I was backslidden for sure.

The peril of looking back is that you end up where you started; your destiny in God is almost destroyed and all the ground you lost you have to make up once you repent. The word of God says this.

> *62 But Jesus said to him, "No one, having put his hand to the plow, and looking back, is fit for the kingdom of God." (Luke 9:62 NKJV)*

Having said that, know that salvation is a process, conceivably deliverance, and healing process in my case, and not a one-off event. Always recognize that your journey of salvation is by Grace and not of your effort. It is not always smooth, glamorous, and interesting, there are times when you lose focus, get tempted and stray from his will, but I'm so glad God died for our past, our present and future sins.

It didn't feel right at all, the mark of God was still on me. The drug addicts would say to me either you're a preacher or a cop and ask me why I would come back out here. I stuck out like a sore thumb. I knew I was wrong on every level. I was a hope to the world. I was doing well when the enemy tricked me, and I went right back to doing what God had delivered me from. My brother came down to live with me and made matters even worse. We were both out there smoking every day he wasn't a good influence at all (Rip Mike) I mean it didn't help that's for sure he was battling his own demons. We were close but being on drugs together was the worst. I wanted to confront him on so many levels especially when he made me mad. He had some serious issues that I don't think he ever got resolved but all was forgiven. He was my brother, but he was the start of my demise from the beginning. I believe he just wanted to be accepted. I learned over the years when you have unforgiveness in your heart and don't forgive people it opens the door for so many other evil spirits to come in. I'm sure he had dealt with some trauma too, or mental illness. You just don't go around touching your little sister. He would always say he was the black sheep of the family. I believe he had a calling on his life, but he never surrendered to God. When he was dying he asked me if he was going to be alright. I said ask God to come into your heart and ask 4 forgiveness.

The Vision of Rapture

I knew I was chosen, and the enemy knew it too. God had a purpose for me and somehow. Even at a young age, I had an encounter with God. I knew it, deep down in my soul. I remember having this dream that woke me up one night.

The rapture had taken place, and it was me and my pastor's brother Denzel we were standing in front of a grocery store, and it looked desolate. One of my best friends Debbie Werth and some other people were caught up in Rapture in the dream the store was unattended. I saw planes in the air crashing into the earth. It was just me and Denzel standing there. We had missed the rapture. Then, I saw big army trucks going by with soldiers in them carrying weapons. I was sitting on the side of the road where they were passing by, then I started walking, I saw a gazebo, and I walked under it. I took two coins out of my pocket which were quarters to get a candy bar out of a machine, a man grabbed my hand, and said your money's no good here. At that moment, I woke up. That dream was on my mind for weeks.

Repentance

I was still getting high, and I knew if I didn't repent, I was going to hell, so I started going back to church but it didn't feel the same. I wasn't out there on the streets for long the second time around, but I left God. It made me feel I couldn't get restored at home because too much damage was done, I felt judged, and I had put God to open shame. I knew too many people, and it was just too much temptation. I talked with my Pastor, and he agreed. So, I moved back to my hometown Cleveland, Ohio in the year 2000. We stayed in touch. I loved my church, and I was homesick, but I knew it was best. I had to get away in a hurry. I left everything, my cars, my clothes; my other kids were pretty much of age by then, so I knew they were okay.

My soul was at stake, and I desperately needed to get back to God. I thank God for my best friend Vanessa. She loved me unconditionally. She was a jewel. I could talk to her about anything and knew she wasn't going to judge me and would just pray. It was hard when I was born in that ministry, and I had built relationships and genuinely loved the folks that had remained. Walking away from God was one of the worst things I could have ever done. I truly missed my family.

I was the most miserable woman. The guilt held onto my mind and heart like a spell. I knew what I had to do. And because I had the word of God living in me, I knew I had to repent. Let me quickly say one thing I learned on this journey is how to be less critical of other people. God taught me a good lesson not to be a finger-pointer as anybody could fall from grace. (Romans 3-23) "For we all have sinned and fall short of the glory of God." I had to learn how to forgive myself. It was Christ's blood then and it was his blood now and he was the only one who could restore me back to himself...

The Interlude

"It was his Blood"

It was his Blood that dripped, as they ravingly pierce his side, it was God who would lay down his life for humanity.

The blood that reaches all life to every high and low mountain, every valley that cleanses our very soul, even in the times of old it, never loses its power.

Oh! How precious is his blood that brought me from a life of sin and shame? How he died for the blind, crippled, lame, and insane

It was his blood that dripped on his garment they ripped and cast lots for, not one mumbling word did he voice.

They gashed a thorn of crown up upon his head, as he bled in sorrow; He kept the world in mind as he suffered in silence and held his peace.

Oh! How precious is our savior's blood, Oh! How precious is our savior's blood?

When I was polluted in my own blood he said to live, his life was the purest thing he could ever give.

I can hear him say Father forgive them because they know not what they do, as he was stretched wide on that rugged cross.

The agony and shame my Lord endured he did it to redeem us back to our rightful place.

He paid the penalty; of sin; he was the judge, juror, and lawyer in every case.

In the garden, you see, when Adam begins to flee, it was the woman you gave Lord, and it was her who had begun to eat.

It is well my sons I paid it in my death, and now you are free.

Oh! How precious is his blood, oh! How precious is our savior's blood?

Oh! How precious is his blood, Oh! How precious is our savior's blood?

God: My children we all must carry our own cross on this journey we call life you see. ('I died for you; now I need you to die for me.")

Your, Heavenly Poet Me.

Chapter 9

A Call to Himself

But know the Lord has set apart him that is godly for himself: the Lord will hear when I call unto him (Psalm 4:3 NKJV)

We packed up, me and my youngest son Deshon and my brother Mike and moved back to Cleveland. I knew right away I had to find a deliverance ministry that preached the truth. I was born out of an apostolic ministry; all I knew was the truth. We were not a perfect church, but we had the love of God and Bishop Bordley made sure we lived up to the name Greater love Temple. I was proud of where I came from.

I always stayed in touch until he passed away. That was a difficult pill to swallow. I knew he was a man after God's own heart. He taught me so much and taught us how to love without hypocrisy.

(RIP) Bishop Curtis Isaiah Bordley

One of his favorite quotes was "You have to be saved twice, once from sin and once from people" I live by that. I'm so delivered from people. He often said "If the devil comes in a wheelchair, kick him over" I registered my son in school, and I began to look for a job. I ended up finding a job at a temporary agency. In between times I started visiting different churches but couldn't really find what I was looking for, I had a preference. It was holiness or nothing. I never liked churches where you had to go through fifty people just to talk to the pastor. We were a close-knit church. So, I was accustomed to certain things.

God Finds Me a Pasture

One morning I went to cash my check and I met a lady who invited me to her church. I told her I came out of an apostolic ministry, and she said that was the type of church she goes to. So, I made plans to go. She picked me up one Sunday. On the way to church, we had a car accident. The enemy didn't want me delivered a second time.

I started attending and God delivered me again through the preached word of God. In retrospect, it became clear to me when the scriptures said in John 15:3. "You are already clean because of the words which I have spoken to you."

I served in that ministry for nine years until the church split because of the fall of our leader. I ended up going to another ministry on the east side of Cleveland under a powerful woman of God. I had never been under a woman leader before because we were taught against it, but it was a wonderful experience and one thing I loved about it is that they believed in prayer. I started going to mid-week prayer and that's when God revealed to me that I was a prophet called by him. I was under her watch care for about five years.

Discipline in Praying my earlier years.

By now I am used to God's voice; I lived with one of the mothers of the church named Mother Carroll back home some years ago, and she taught me how to pray and how important it was to spend time with God. I mean every morning she would stand at the bottom of the stairs and call my name. There was no getting around it. We had to get up for devotion@ 5am every morning. Don't get me wrong we were a praying church too. For me, this was another new experience of fellowship with God. It was truly a sacrifice.

I was like, can't I just pray in my bed? Didn't you say God was omnipresent? Of course, I said that under my breath, there wasn't any way I was saying that to her face. It taught us discipline.

My Godson had it bad and he never wanted to get up for prayer so he would get up, go to the bathroom, run the water in the sink and go to sleep on the bathroom floor. All I would hear was Joshua! Joshua! His grandmother called his name and we didn't start until he came out. Those were the good old days. I told you nobody was escaping 5 a.m. prayer; it was for eternity.

We chuckled about it from time to time. We knew how important prayer was and spending time with God, and because of it my entire life is dedicated to prayer. A true mother of zion It was like God anointed her voice just to call people or something, she was a praying woman, I mean every single morning without missing a day. It was time I said okay maybe she overslept today, that didn't happen ever. She was just so disciplined.

It didn't matter who stayed over, you were hitting the bricks baby. It was a short time we lived together. Our routine was getting up reading the scripture, and then praying. It was then I learned intimacy with God and developed a prayer life that stuck with me until this very day. She was the one who instilled that in me, her children, grandchildren, and great-grandchildren. I was blessed to be a part of that time. I was her spiritual daughter, and I love her dearly. I might not have agreed with everything she did, but we had to respect our elders. My spiritual father made sure of it, whether they were right or wrong there was no talking back. I didn't grow up with parents so some things I had to learn even as an adult. Bishop Bordley taught us discipline and respect through the word of God which was what the scriptures say in Ephesian 6:1-4 about honoring your mother and father and that wasn't just your natural parents but, it was the spiritual ones too. We had to respect our elders.

I believe she is about eighty-six years old today and still rises at the same time every morning. I have called her and had devotions even now. There's something unique about the 5am prayer and seeking God's face early in the morning. Those mothers walked in power and could get a prayer through to God. You hear me. We need power restored back in the church.

The Prophetic Call Revealed

It was a Tuesday morning in a prayer meeting. The Spirit of God fell on me so heavily. He said noticeably I'm calling you as a prophet to the nations. I said yes, Lord, and I just wept in his presence. I felt it was an honor to speak for God. It wasn't long after that, God put me on a thirty-day sabbatical, I told my leader at the time she agreed, and God never allowed me to return. He was calling me out. I was there for five years. Instantly after God released me he began to deal with me from that point on.

The Lord spoke to me and said, "I'm going to do more for you than what you're getting when you come down here for prayer. I said yes Lord I was nervous but I obeyed. I knew God had me in that ministry for a reason, and it was to pray. But he called me out and started dealing with me in prayer. He said I'm calling you to myself without further interruption. I said yes Lord. Then he said, now, this is the time I want you to get up and start seeking me he gave me a specific time to get into his presence, and this happened for at least six months straight. This was all new to me. I had never been out of church for an extended period. It made me nervous, but I was happy at the same time. I just needed a break. I was tired anyway of what I had just experienced from the previous church I left. I came from a true man of God so my expectations were high. He had such a balance, he was a stern man but he had the true love of God and we loved and respected him dearly. He was truly called to pastored God's people. He used to say to us over the pulpit everybody weighs one pound. One thing I respected about him was he pastored most of his family and never showed any favoritism ever, although me and his nephew tabu thought we were his favorite in our mind. He is truly missed. After being called by God, I remember listening to Juanita Bynum one night, she preached a message "It's Time to go" when I finished listening to that message, I knew God was talking to me, and I felt settled in my spirit.

God gives instructions.

God had begun to talk to me about things I had never heard before. He was teaching me and stretching me on a whole different level, and I was falling more in love with him by the minute.

By that time, I didn't care what anybody thought. He was God, and he was in control of my life. He was dealing with me quickly and rapidly. When I first moved into my house, I turned one of my bedrooms into my prayer room, and I made sure nobody went in and out but me. I prayed in that room for 8 years and God would meet me there in my secret place. He said to me, "I am the school of the prophets sit at my feet and I will teach you."

First, he really began developing my hearing; the more I stayed in prayer talking to God the more I understood what he was doing. I was pregnant spiritually and had to be birthed out for a purpose. Again, I was travailing. By the middle or the end of 2016, I went to visit a church on the east side of Cleveland. They called themselves a spiritual church that operated in prophetic gifts, something I was a novice to at the time I was just learning and coming into what God had called me to. .

It was back home we would have a man of God come through to preach and prophesy every now, and then. We really didn't work in the gifts of the Holy Spirit, and it really wasn't taught as much as it was learning to just live Holy. We didn't even believe in women preachers, pastors, in ministry, but I remembered him prophesying to me, and he said your ministry is far beyond these four walls. I didn't understand it then, but it all became clear later. On my first visit I enjoyed myself dearly; however, what really caught my attention was the way he taught the word of God. It was fresh manna from heaven. Stuff my ears had never heard before. I was tuned in, and he was also a prophet of God.

I really learned about who I was, and what God had called me to do. That I was a prophet to the nations, the Lord had me praying quite a bit, and he was doing all the pouring, and man the stuff I heard in those dimensions I'm still in awe. "How unsearchable are his judgments, and his ways past finding out" Romans 11:33). I will get to what he revealed later in the chapters to come. He was revealing secrets and strategies that I surely needed up the road. I was in a fight for my life. The warfare was real, and the enemy was trying to knock the wind out of me. I had never experienced warfare like what i had encountered ever.

He didn't want me to get to the next level of my spiritual journey and training. I was learning new things through revelation, the preached word of God, and prayer. What I came to realize was that I was bound by the Spirit of religion and sitting under the man of God allowed me to get free in that ministry.

Delivered From the Tradition of Men

I was there for about two years. It was around 2016 – 2018. I never joined because I wasn't led to. But it was family. I remember the man of God would allow me to pray over the services, he was the first person who gave me a chance to preach God's word. I was set free from the shackles of religion. I knew what order was because I was always taught that. I liked what I heard, and I was taken in by the word of God, not the rules. I finally got free looking back; I was saved yet bound by tradition in the church. I'm sure the way we were taught wasn't all wrong, but a lot of things weren't right either. What I'm trying to say is some things I was taught some time ago and my views have changed drastically. It was just the way we were taught it's what I needed at that time; I came right out of the streets. It was my foundation that's why I'm alive today. We learned character, that's what's missing in the body of Christ today. We have witnessed excellent demonstrations of gifts and talents but not character. We were taught to always stand on the truth.

God is doing a new thing and if the church doesn't grab it or get hold of it, we are really going to miss the move of God. Well, what are we talking about? Remember Pastors pretty much told us how to think. We didn't have an opinion, we just had to obey. There you have it. If God gave us a mind and free will, who's to control that but him? The Bible says, "Obey them that have rule over you" Hebrews 13:17. I'm not talking about the word of God. But, man theory, religion, church doctrines, men and their tradition, there is truly a difference. It has become spiritual abuse. I was ordained and able to attain my minister's license through that ministry, and I was so grateful.

I enjoyed being there. I started learning a little about the prophetic. I didn't denounce the spiritual teaching I received years back, I just denounced religion. We had an enjoyable time; the service was great and vibrant. I was learning and growing, and seeing things from a different perspective. My eyes were enlightened by so many new things, and I just enjoyed learning.

My ears were tired of the same old thing; I was already getting bored in church. I wanted to go higher in God, and God wanted to take me there. The scriptures teach, in Matthew 5:6 "Blessed are those who hunger and thirst for righteousness, for they shall be filled." I knew there was more to God than just being saved, sanctified, and filled with the Holy Ghost. I wanted revelations, mysteries, and the depth of God- I just wanted to experience the deep thing of God. I just knew it was more to this Big God. Juanita Bynum quoted "Information without revelation is stagnation" I told God I never want to be that kind of preacher and some things I wasn't going to denounce and that was order, honoring leadership, sanctification, and standing on truth forever.

Stepping Out Into Ministry

I was nobody's fool, I was a praying woman, and I knew the voice of God. But the spirit of tradition kept us from enjoying Jesus and the new life in Christ. During this time, God birthed a prayer line through me. 5 a.m. prayer called the "Gathering of the Warriors." God was doing some remarkable things with us on the line. People were healed, set free, and delivered. He would take us into realms in the Spirit that was unquestionable. I believe God had me birthing out some other prophet on the line, and now they are walking in their God-given purpose.

Later the prayer ministry turned into The "Gathering of Warriors prophetic Conferences."

Prayer was my life and God kept revealing himself in unusual ways and my love for him grew deeper. One thing I've learned is that it takes sacrifice and dedication. What are you willing to sacrifice? Had to ask myself that question until God told me what he thought. All I know God was doing the pouring and nobody gets credit for that but God. During this year, my prayer life was very intense. He had me praying three times a day, which was three hours a day. I had never prayed for that many hours on a consistent basis. Trust me, I found out later why it was so necessary. I remember God asked me. "Do you want your Ministry to be great or mediocre? I said great Lord, he said I need you to separate. I had to shut down to what was familiar. I had to cut off old friends, I remember God telling me he did not want everyone to be so accessible to me. I mean I went cold turkey. It was an adjustment period for sure and extremely uncomfortable, I had never experienced this before, just me and God. Nonetheless, one thing I know is that my new destiny has God's signature on it. He was crossing me over and a new birth was taking place.

The Discipline of Obedience

I had to eventually let that prayer line go. Cut some folks off and die some more to the flesh to crossover.

I would come home from work at 7am shower and head to my prayer chamber. I was in prayer at 9 a.m. then at 12 a.m. then, at 3 p.m. and this went on for an exceptionally long time, I mean months, even until this day when he instructed me. God was doing something for me that I will never forget. In prayer he told me he was going to do an overhaul on my body in the year of 2016. He would begin to download things from heaven. I was enjoying this new level in God, but then, it came with so much warfare and a price. One thing God was teaching me was separation. It was hard at first, but I stayed in the face of God. He was preparing me for something great! He started talking to me in codes and strategies unheard of, this was unbelievable. I mean when I tell you I was amazed, I truly was. I kept going to church on Sundays, still fasting and praying. I would work at night from 11 p.m. to 7 a.m. And was able to pray at the appointed time God wanted me to pray.

I knew I heard God's voice when he told me he was calling me to Himself. I had no choice. I was scared, and felt all alone, again I felt like Joseph I was in the place of God. But felt like John the Baptist on the isle of Patmos (Revelation 1:9). Obedience is a lonely place, don't ever forget it. It's still lonely. I was in isolation for a long period of time. I didn't have friends and trying to explain what God was doing was hopeless, especially talking to people about what God was doing and what he was birthing out. A couple years passed.

I remember telling God I was so lonely, not for a man but

just friends. The Lord said to me, " I will keep you company now go in the kitchen make yourself a cup of tea and come and sit with me. I got up, went into the kitchen, made myself a cup of tea, came back and sat down in my chair in the living room. It was from that day on I really never felt lonely again at that magnitude, as time went on, I understood why. What I can add to my resume is that I know God as a Comforter now.

While I was praying God began to change my diet, certain things I could not eat. He would tell me exactly what I could eat and couldn't eat. It took a lot of discipline. I'm not saying it was easy all the time, it was a struggle, anything you had a habit of doing for years is always hard to break, sometimes I failed, but I started seeing the importance of it later down the road I just stopped eating meat. He began to reveal what was in chicken and what was in beef and just told me secrets about what we were putting in our bodies and gave me secrets and remedies in prayer on what to put in my body especially when I became sick. I was going through a spiritual detox.

What God was doing was to get me into a place of discipline in my life and get me healthy spiritually and naturally. I remember him speaking to me and his exact words were "I died for you, and now I need you to die for me." That statement blew my wig back. Then, I knew that something else in me had to die, and this flesh had to come under subjection. Now I had to deal with being alone on a whole different level. I was always a loner. I was never a crowd chaser. This is because I was continuously rejected but all the time connected to God and that's all that mattered. I was in a Spiritual quarantine even before the pandemic started.

God Drawing Me Closer

I was like Jesus Christ on the mount of transfiguration Matthew 17. I was learning so many new things, but it only happened through obedience. I knew it was something different going on. A lot that God showed me came through prayer. He was preparing and maturing me in some areas of the inner man and doing a lot of purging and developing me in the prophetic, and sending me out on assignments. I didn't know it but I was starting to walk into what he called me into and learning about me.

I told the Lord I will go where you send me, and I will say what you ask me to say. I still tell God this today, and I truly mean it in my heart. One night the Lord spoke to me "he said they are going to think you're crazy like they did Jeremiah, the prophet when you start to declare what God was saying." This could mean in my future ministry.

When I got up from praying I would just sit or lay there and ponder on those things in my heart as Mary did in Luke 2:19. If I had told anyone what God said or showed me, nobody would believe me. They would think I was crazy. One day, I was in prayer and the Lord said these exact words to me. "Let me introduce myself! I'm God." My response in my Spirit, did you just say that to me?" I have never heard anything like that in all my saved life. I guess God was reintroducing himself to me a second time on a whole new level. I was fine with that because he was teaching who he really was, and I had to learn how to trust him on this new level. I love the time I spend with God and my intimacy with him. I ask the Lord to tell me things you don't tell everybody else. Then, God replies "can you keep a secret?" My reply was yes Lord, then he would begin to speak.

Those are just some of the sweet intimate conversations we had. God was aligning me and getting me ready for his purpose through separation, dedication, fasting, and praying. It was so much birth out of me in the last four years, but the more he poured out and revealed the more I hungered for his presence and that has never left me. I always have a special love for God and being set apart came with a lot of suffering. Salvation is free but the oil cost. My faith was on trial and I became his friend.

The Fragrance of God

His scent was all on me, and I was really being transformed into his perfect image Romans 12:2, and another level of his glory was being revealed. It was his doing, and he was getting all the glory. My prayer life continued the more I prayed and read the more I learned about him, and I enjoyed every moment he cared enough about me to bring me close and sit me right at his feet. I was like Mary, who sat at Jesus's feet listening to what he said, Luke 10:38-42. I chose the good part that will never be taken away. God was dealing with me in such a profound way I was learning things about God I don't believe any man could have taught me in all respect. I believe I was at that ministry for about two years until I moved on from there.

I started visiting other places by the leading of the Lord but was still staying in the face of God. I knew my boundaries if God said no, I didn't go. By this time, I was free, so I wasn't for any junk. I was tired of the shenanigans, and past disappointments from church leaders. I just wanted God from the very beginning when he saved me in 1989. I was free from people free from religion, and there was no way I was going back into bondage. I meant every bit of it doesn't matter where God sent me. Believe me, people were cemented in this stuff. I could smell it a mile a minute only because I was free now. I'm calling it how I see it. It was tradition, religion, and control.

That's one thing Bishop Jones said, don't let any damned preachers take you back there. He wasn't cursing, read the word he was just saying the truth, and he wanted to make sure I heard him loud and clear... Dammed, being lost, Jesus said in Mark 7:8 you disregard the commandments of God and cling faithfully to the traditions of men. Jesus was making a statement but being a little sarcastic too. "The traditions of men"

Going on Assignments for God.

One thing I admired about him was he didn't give a hill of beans what anybody thought about him. When I left that ministry in

2018, God would begin to send me on assignments in the city that same year. I remember visiting a church God sent me to and God used me one day. I laid hands on five people, and they were filled with the Holy Ghost God had me to pray for this young lady.. I remember laying hands on a young lady God told me she had a spirit of suicide on her. God told me to cast that spirit out of her, I obeyed the Spirit of God, and she got delivered. God was really moving, and I was excited about what he was doing through me. I just genuinely wanted to please God and stay in his perfect will. I believe my ministry is in deliverance. The enemy was mad so of course I went through a lot of persecution.

I never stayed; I just went when God told me to go. It was from there I started going to another church under another leader in late 2018 until 2019 by the leading of the Lord. A prophet told me to get under someone, of course I prayed. I felt maybe this was it. I truly had a love for the people of God. God said I'm sending you in as a sniper. It was an inside job to go in the Spirit of love. On this journey I have been attacked by witches and warlocks you name it; listen Jezebel is not a woman wearing red lipstick chasing after pastors that spirit hides in many forms.

I needed to go under submission, I didn't quite understand until I obeyed. I was there for three reasons: to be covered, to expose and to be healed. Sometimes a soldier must go in to retreat to gain strength when he's hit too many times in the battle. Not knowing sometimes it's the Generals that are trying to kill you, but It was all for my making.

It Is a Learning Expedition

Don't get me wrong everywhere God sent me was an experience of learning, the lessons I learned were what not to do and what to do in the ministry. With the strategies God taught me in prayer, I was able to withstand the warfare. The enemy was mad at me, but I kept going as God led me despite people's opinions of me and what they said. It makes me wonder how in tune people were with God's voice. I was in training... It was good for a minute and things started to go left.

Things misinterpreted:

In 2019, after my prophetic conference, I left and made a transition under another leader for almost a year until the middle of 2020 by God's leading. That was by far my hardest assignment ever, but I passed the test. The places God sent me were for my training and testing. I'm so glad I made it through. They say Prophets are often misunderstood but they were right, I experienced it. Firsthand the persecution, the lies, and the betrayal, but the lesson I learned and the testing I went through strengthened me and enlarged my borders.

I was in training camp being conditioned for ministry up the road. I was there to pray and to be a witness and more development. I remember one Sunday morning lifting my hands in worship, I heard the Lord say, so clearly it was mechanical. I knew what he meant. Everything was controlled so I could not worship freely. I was sick to my belly. I loved to praise him but give me worship any day. I was ready to leave, but God said not yet. The Lord revealed to me that it was STRANGE FIRE and that's what's going on in these churches today. A gift without sanctification and purification is dangerous. I heard this song...

"Oh! zion what's the matter now" You don't sing like you used to sing, You don't pray like you used to pray, you dont preach like you used to preach, what's the matter now..Oh! zion what's the matter now.

I'm secure in who I am, and it took me a long time to get here, and nobody is knocking me off my square not this time or making me feel like I'm anything less than what God says I am.

I'm moving to destiny. There is an oil spill about to happen; you gotta catch that one in the Spirit. The enemy was mad because God was exposing and showing me things so I wouldn't be deceived and furthermore, I wasn't going back into bondage. I never had a problem with submitting, that's the first thing people like to say nobody wants to submit to leadership, my answer is no nobody wants to be controlled by a spirit of witchcraft.

I'm so glad that from time to time God would send me to a church on the west side of Cleveland, it was a house of REFUGE for me, and it was where I would go and get strength and regroup. Every so often the Apostle would counsel me and encourage me. One of my favorite preachers in the city (NBM) Then God told me to go under a Woman Apostle that had moved out of town and pay tithes into that ministry and I obeyed.

I did that by zooming but it was refreshing. I felt I was safe and could breathe for a moment. I wasn't going to be judged but really covered. By the end of October God released me. He said I'm enlarging your capacity and I knew what that meant. When God released me, a young prophet gave a word that my prayer life was going higher, and God told me that he was sending me on a hundred-day threshing floor experience and this time it was going to be different.

I was expecting God to do something great and had expectations like never before. I was excited; it was going to be even more than what he had already downloaded, but it came with a price. God was gracing me. It was my alone time with God that was priceless. I wouldn't trade it for anything. It was the intimacy with God that kept me, as long as I could hear from God I was okay. I was going from glory to glory.

Chapter 10

MY HUNDRED-DAY THRESHING FLOOR EXPERIENCE

The threshing floors will be filled with grain; the vats will overflow with new wine and oil **Joel 2:24 - NIV**

That's when I started to set my heart toward God to spend more time before the Lord, even more. But, what was my Threshing floor? All I knew was that it was a place of revelation and detachment. Where the harvest was prepared by separating the grain from the unusable straw for the purpose of uncovering and saving the most valuable part of the crop, at least that's what the google definition was but let's get the real meaning.

As the name suggests threshing floor according to the

scriptures is usually a place most likely isolated where harvested grains are tramped to separate the chaff covering them and the stalk on which they are held. Separating the grain from the chaff and stalk exposes the valuable part of the crops normally the seed. Threshing on the other hand is the act of applying pressure on the grain to separate them from the fodders. Threshing can be done by tramping on the grain using the feet or by using animals such as cattle, donkeys, or horses to tramp out the grain from stalks.

Interpreting and appropriating this meaning to us as Christians, the Threshing floor is that reasonably isolated place or environment where God communicates with you as an individual. Whereas, on the other hand, threshing is the process of separating or dedicating yourself to God and allowing God to remove and replace certain aspects in you for the purpose of His kingdom and bringing out His divine nature in you as seen in (John 15:1-8). The threshing floor is an exclusive habitation where we separate and dedicate our life to God, it is a place of revelation and discovery where we allow God to dress or refine us, and so we can fit into His purpose. I perceive in my spirit that everyone needs a threshing floor experience; Jesus Christ was away for forty (40) days and forty (40) nights in the wilderness. He didn't go there for fun, picnic, or because he was on vacation. The scriptures said he was led by the Holy Spirit (Luke 4:1-13).

Have you ever wondered why Jesus Christ always moves

away from the crowd and even his disciples to the mountains or a noiseless atmosphere to pray? As recorded in the following scriptures (Luke 22:39-46; Luke 6:12; Matthew 14:23) Praying in serene places wasn't a one-off activity for Jesus Christ the scriptures said, as his custom was.

> *39 Coming out, He went to the Mount of Olives, as He was accustomed, and His disciples also followed Him. 40 When He came to the place, He said to them, "Pray that you may not enter into temptation." 41 And He was withdrawn from them about a stone's throw, and He knelt down and prayed* **(Luke 22:39-41 NKJV)**

In my mind I believe God was drawing me into my death experience, which meant that the flesh had to be crucified and obedience had to spring forth. The flesh had to be crucified and obedience had to spring forth.

As I have come to discover, once you encounter God at that level sweetheart, nothing else could ever do. Fellowships with God in a tranquil environment, allow you to hear God clearly because distractions are reduced.

The Refining

As the Lord needed to work out something in my life I had to go through the process of some more refining. It didn't start until the second month at the top of the year, God had already prepared me. I was already praying three times a day not really knowing what was going to take place while on my threshing floor. The first thing the Lord told me was that this threshing floor experience was going to be very different. First, he instructed me to detox my body. I was already eating correctly because he had already changed my diet, yet I had to detox (purify). I was in another spiritual quarantine, When you eat light you hear right. How about Daniel? (Daniel 1:8-21) Daniel was ten times wiser because he honored God with his life and what he put in his body. He didn't bow to the king and didn't eat his portion of meat.

I had never been introduced to this level of prayer and intimate relationship and fellowship with God and learning about what it meant to be in the presence of the highest. I'm so glad God took me this way. I learned God on a whole different level, it was my process and God was fine-tuning me like I said the warfare was getting very intense, I was dying out and still pushing past some challenges. I was still dealing with being separated. As I said previously, obedience is a lonely place. He was allowing me to know the difference and teaching me some things about him.

The Enemy Struck in 2020

That same year I caught COVID and got so sick, it was an experience I will never forget. I had some difficult days. That's when this thing hit our nation and the world was in fear; however, on December 5, 2019 I will never forget that morning in prayer the Lord said pronounce to the people that there is an economic collapse coming and resources will be dried up. By January 2020 it was right in our faces and the nation was on edge. It was the month of September God started dealing with me in a very unusual way. I was still praying three times a day and fasting, he was preparing me for what I didn't know.

It was November 22, 2020, when I contracted COVID. I was fearful. I didn't know what to expect. I had never been sick like this. I remember sitting in bed dealing with the symptoms, I mean this thing hit me hard. The Lord gave me Psalm 91 to stand on. I would read it every day, even when the spirit of fear came to take my mind. Things became bleak in a moment. I was so sick this went on for about the first two weeks. It truly was a trying time, and He wouldn't allow me to talk to anybody because I was still in a spiritual quarantine. It was something I had to go through by myself.

I remember I heard the Lord say it is a spirit of death on me; I jumped up and went into the living room. He told me to get on Facebook and tell the people to repent. I could barely breathe at this point. It was a little while after that, I called the ambulance, but before that, I heard such a thump in my body. It was so noticeable that I stopped what I was doing, and asked myself what was that? I was rushed to the hospital; they told my sister I had COded. I didn't remember anything.

My Testimony

All I remember was I had double pneumonia. I was admitted for seven days. I remember lying in that hospital bed talking to God and asking Him "God you said you had an arsenal of weapons. How do I fight now?" I had just preached a message titled Approved weapons. I began to tell God what was going on with my body as if he didn't already know. I said Lord my heart, he said I'm cleaning out your arteries, I said what about my colon he said I'm cleaning out your colon too. He said to me I'm putting cartilage back in your knee, I am giving you a blood transfusion also, and I am healing your shoulder. What an awesome God. He healed me supernaturally by his power just like he promised me four years prior. He told me he was doing an overhaul on my body. He said I'm giving you a clean bill of health. The process of my healing started while I was laying in that hospital bed.

He always keeps his promises, I went into my prayer room to worship, an appearance of a rainbow appeared on the wall not one not two but three. I was amazed it was undeniable. I stared at that rainbow for at least thirty minutes and took a picture. I walked outside to see if it was raining or something. I was in amazement, it was in the same spot I sat and worshiped for days as God had instructed me. Our God is a covenant keeper (see the picture at the back of the book).

He told me five years prior he was going to do an overhaul on my body that will take me back to my youthful days and add years to my life. Confirming what the scriptures said;

I shall not die, but live, and declare the works of the Lord (psalms 118-17).

This must have been the start of the process of my overhaul naturally, and spiritually I reasoned. Nonetheless, I didn't know that it was coming through my sickness then he began to deal with me about what was coming to this nation and about the vaccine.

I began to weep in that hospital bed and thank my Father in Heaven; I didn't know how I was going to make it. They wanted to send me to rehabilitation but I had no insurance, God said I said "you're going." I went for fourteen days. Truly I was thankful I had prayers stored up with God and some fasting too, only God knew what was coming. My lungs were not doing well so after being hospitalized that's why they sent me to rehab because of pneumonia, besides I was on sick leave from my job.

My insurance had run out and had no income coming in. I had used all my sick days, so I didn't know what to do and on top of that God told me not to return because he was sending judgment to that place. I was in a place of despair, then I got a call from my supervisor, a week later and she said they were giving each employee a COVID relief bonus which was about four thousand dollars. All I could do was thank God.

My two grandchildren Sophia and Sydney contracted COVID from me. They were with me before I got tested. I really was on edge. This was a hard place to trust God, nevertheless, he was my help and my stay Psalm 33:20, and He was making a way Isaiah 43:16-19; 1 Corinthians 10:13. I was really concerned about my grandchildren, but they came through. In rehabilitation, the Lord used me to witness to some people. A lady gave her life to Christ. God told me to pray for a woman who came in with COVID. He said she wasn't going to make it through the night if I didn't pray for her. So, I got out of bed and obeyed God. I was praying and prophesying all while recovering myself in the rehab. We were all on the COVID unit and God had some sweet people take care of me. They would sometimes come into my room just to talk about how good God was.

Satan Struck Again

I was finally released and was home for about two weeks. Then, I fell sick again. I almost passed out in my home. I went back to the hospital about five or six times after that, something just didn't feel right. This went on for two weeks straight. I couldn't put my finger on it. I finally called my doctor, and they told me to come in. I drove myself to the clinic. I remember the Lord told me to get up and walk about thirty minutes a day when I was in the hospital the first time. I did the best I could but, looking back I saw why he told me to do so.

When I got there my heart rate was 120 beats per minute, they called the ambulance right away, and she said your heart is running a marathon. She was nervous herself. When I got there, they admitted me and found two blood clots in my lungs. I spent another seven days in the hospital. I was going through it, you hear me, but God brought me out after being released. My body was going through what they called the long haul my body was going through so many changes I thought I was literally losing my mind. For several days I cried and cried after a while, the Lord said I'm going to renew your strength Isaiah 40:31. He did just that. It was a lengthy process he started to deal with me about the "Seven stages of healing." I will save that for another time.

My Body Playing Tricks

My body was playing tricks on me, I couldn't explain it. For days, I couldn't get out of bed because I was so weak. I started having panic attacks and anxiety attacks, out of nowhere and couldn't talk to anyone, something I never went through in my life, though I have been in some dark places. I didn't know what was going on. This went on for a long time. The enemy was trying to take my mind, but God prevented it. I contracted COVID in 2020 until the whole year 2021. I was down and still going through some challenges in 2022, then I had to get two biopsies on my throat because of my thyroid. I thank God for a leader I was under the Lord led him to pray for my throat, as I went in to get the biopsies one side was undetermined, they wanted me to have surgery. I battled with that decision for a while. It wasn't until I went to a service one night and the worship was so high in that place when I lifted my hands, I heard the Lord say let me do the surgery.

I had only been hospitalized when I gave birth to my kids. I prayed and didn't really know which way to go. I finally had surgery and the Lord said to me you're coming out with a clean getaway and he brought me out. It was a cancerous tumor they took out, they said it was nonaggressive, and I would still be under my doctor's care" Then they diagnosed me with degenerative bone disease, and God gave me strategies on what to do. He's restoring my bones, then was diagnosed with stage two kidney disease. He is restoring me just like he promised.

It was such a trying time, I thought I was going crazy so many things and challenges were going on in my mind and body and I couldn't explain it to anyone. I didn't know myself. It was many days I cried and cried and cried out to God. I thought I would never get better. Mind you I have not worked because I wasn't able to for two years straight going on three but God is yet providing for me.

Looking back over my life, I have never been sick in all the fifty-nine years of my life. What a mighty God we serve. Restoration is my portion of God that has made me completely whole. I'm truly healed by faith. I have so much work to do for the kingdom of God. I have healed well from my thyroid surgery and because they only removed half I don't have to be on medicine for the rest of my life. I give all glory to God. I remember God saying to me, I will let you know when to go to a doctor. He put them here for a reason. Sometimes healing comes through medicine, but I won't ever forget who the chief physician is and that is God.

Divine Restoration

It took a while for me just to feel normal again. Every time I thought I was getting better something else would happen. My God i thought it was over for me but i kept fighting i kept hoping and asking God is this it Lord?

The Lord spoke to me and said don't let the enemy steal your healing, so I had to fight through some things in my own mind. It was some difficult days and nobody really to talk to and confide in was truly hard. My heart was heavy and I thought I would never get better. I had to come to grips with some things concerning people, sometimes you wonder where all the people are you helped in the past and now when you needed help the most, you couldn't find them anywhere, even with family I'm telling you I had a difficult time excepting some people behavior.

I asked the Lord where the love of God was through people when I needed them the most. The lord spoke to me and said I'm elevating your love and I was wondering why my love needed to be elevated. I didn't have a problem so I thought I was angry. Sometimes you have to continue to love no matter what, and never expect people to be you and some things I just had to accept even with family. What God taught me was to learn to depend on him and to have faith in him only. I guess where I came from we were taught agape love we went to see about people.

I recall just trying to feel better and get back to myself, but it wasn't working. It was the strangest thing I have ever endured; I recollect asking God what was that thump that I heard and felt in my body before I was rushed to the hospital. God spoke to me and said that it was me restarting your heart. He told me to take it easy and wanted me to rest, it was just like I had a heart transplant. My God I just wanted to get well but God wanted my body to rest.

Eventually, I was getting my strength back and getting back to my normal self. It was truly a journey that I'm still walking through day by day. My Threshing floor was supposed to start at the top of the year of 2021, but God didn't allow it to happen until the month of March. I began to get really back into the presence of God daily, sometimes three times a day as before. When I had the strength, he started giving me new strategies. This time it was different just like he said, I knew something had changed. I was in such a different realm and on a new level with God. I was living in a place in the Spirit and of course, I felt those gravitational pulls from time to time. He allowed me to visit those places in spirit, it was phenomenal. I remember lying on my couch reading about Apostle Paul and the third heavens 2 Corinthians 12:1-4. God said to me he went to an atmosphere. I was just amazed it was just so much about God I wanted and yearned to know.

The Vision After Twenty-One Day Fast

My faith was still on trial, but God was my stay! He told me to go on a twenty-one-day fast and gave me instructions on what to do. That's when I really got the true meaning of fasting; we have had it all wrong for years, at least some of us. There were more revelations. I went over twenty-one days and found myself in my prayer room dehydrated and almost ended up back in the hospital. This was the beginning of my threshing floor yet, I was fasting here and there when God said, but prayer never ceased. I finally came off the twenty-one days. I had overstretched my body, God said, so you went over and beyond, and then he put strength back in me. I didn't want to go back to the hospital and I remember getting up and drinking as much as I could but it took a couple of days to get my strength back. My entire life has been dedicated to fasting and praying.

It was maybe two weeks later I heard in prayer. God said it was about to be combustion, and I had no idea what God was trying to communicate to me, all I knew was when I looked up the word in the Webster dictionary the meaning was, a chemical reaction between two substances. Maybe, it was me, and God I had no clue what he was up to, but I found out. It was near the end of the week and I heard the lord say this week will be very challenging for you. I didn't know what to expect, I was trying to prepare but still I didn't know what was coming. I heard the word dig right after that.

The Vision of the jackhammer.

I saw this jackhammer and a big drill in a vision when I was praying, then I saw a huge bulldozer digging up dirt. I saw dirt on the top of this big hole and when it was moved back to the bottom, I saw oil. The hole was deep. I heard these words "let me dig my daughter." I said yes Lord and still didn't know what he meant in fullness. Perhaps I was about to strike oil or something. It was that Sunday after church I had to get ready for a seven day isolation. I was about to go under.

Seven Days in His Presence

The instructions came, and he said to me, turn off the TV, turn off the phone, and cut off all outside communication for seven days straight. Do not answer any calls, no texting I couldn't even look at the phone. no computer, nothing. He wanted my undivided attention and total silence. What? Omg Lord: right there was a rough week. I was just wondering how I was going to get through it without the TV. I know I need some deliverance right? That was my past time. I didn't know what to expect. I was going into solitary confinement. I'm telling you seven days straight. That was the longest week in history. This was still part of my hundred-day threshing floor. It wasn't easy being in total confinement again.

It was a challenging week for real, but it was worth the sacrifice and being obedient was good. I challenge anyone to try it with no phone, no tv, no computer, no communication with no one and besides having to stay in one room, I couldn't come out but to eat and to use the bathroom for seven days straight. This was the first time God told me to do anything like this.

I had to get my mind prepared for this. I was nervous about whether I could complete this task, but something in me was telling me to obey God, besides I hated disappointing God.

My First Day - Monday 9 a.m. Prayer

He instructed me to start praying in all white, so I got some all-white garments anointed them, and have been praying in these sacred garments ever since, then he said to me get some frankincense and burn it as they did in the temple. I believe it all started on that Monday morning at about 9am in prayer, I began to see that same vision of a deep hole in the ground, a treasure chest with chains as before in this hole, and an angel pulling it up out of the hole. The Lord begins to speak to me and said I'm about to allow you to dig up some treasures. I had never experienced this before in my life, this vision was real. The treasure chest was up, and the angel opened it. In it were precious jewels. He said to me It's about to be an explosion in the Spirit. He said to me, I need you to document times and seasons. I began to see some deep wells in a reservoir like an oasis, then I saw rivers. I started writing.

The Same Day 6 P.M. Prayer

I laid out prostrate on my prayer room floor, pondering on what I had seen in the previous vision earlier. I heard God say to me, I'm going to give you the blueprint, and I am going to show you how to get there. He said you're about to strike gold. I found myself digging again and this time I saw deep wells and another treasure chest, and the angel of the Lord brought it up to the earth. I opened it. There were two beautiful purple scarves. They were beautiful like royalties. Another treasure chest was brought up from the earth; it was filled with maps, blueprints, manuscripts, and books. It was about eight treasure chests altogether.

Day 2 - Tuesday 9 A.M. Prayer

I laid out before God and kept quiet in his presence, then he spoke, just call it unusual what was about to happen. "I'm taking you higher daughter" then I remember I was standing on top of a mountain, and I could see the world. He said, "You're about to have a mountaintop experience, signs, wonders, and miracles." I had to stay in his presence if you have ever been in a place like this; you just know you better not disobey God. This was a command I had to obey his voice. He said, "I'm bridging the gap.

You are about to start building your legacy and I'm about to bless you beyond measure you're about to walk in your destiny."

The Same Day 3 P.M. Prayer

"There will be no miss fire, every place in your life is about to be watered," God was ready to get me in total alignment with his perfect will. He is going to cause my hands to prosper. I am the way the truth and life (John 14:6). He said, "Keep digging" I began to descend into this deep hole, and I saw another treasure chest, then I saw musical notes I started to write, it was the jingle to a production God had given me some years earlier, by this time I was in amazement I took a book and began to write the music chords in a book. He spoke to me and said, "You are a creative genius." He said, "I have placed a writing anointing upon you."

The Same Day 6 P.M. Prayer

I started to see an alabaster box with oil in it. I heard God say "my scent is all over you." He said, "You're in the birth canal of God. I'm changing your ear frequencies, so you will begin to hear sounds from heaven. Earth-shattering sounds." Then, I saw beautiful artifacts I was going to obtain that were very expensive pictures and paintings.

Day 3 - Wednesday 9 A. M. Prayer

I missed prayer due to my working over when we got mandated

that morning at work. This was the third day of my threshing floor experience. I had to stay in prayer and my focus was on God, but my flesh was crying out for the carnal, but I stayed my course. I came home from work and showered, set my alarm, and was up at 3 p.m. for prayer.

The Same Day 3 P.M. Prayer

I heard the Lord say, "it is well, stay focused. He is going to allow me to see His Glory." I see two more treasure chests. Then, I heard God say "go up to the mount there is a supernatural transformation coming." I'm telling you about my supernatural experiences with God; I never wanted it to end. Again, the spirit was willing but the flesh was weak (Matthew 26:41). Can you imagine Moses up on the mount with God forty days and forty nights? (Exodus 19:20; Exodus 34:28). I was having that wow moment. I don't know what happened after that, I just remember waking up stretched out on the floor.

The same day 6 p.m. prayer

I began to pray and listen to what God had to say. By this time I just wanted to see what God had for me next. I remember that evening I came out of the presence of God and he said the angels want to come visit you. I was speechless. I couldn't believe what God was saying to me. Would you mind if they came? I hesitated and God said no you wouldn't' mind. I said no Lord. I was in awe especially if you never had any experiences like this ever it was awesome.

Day 4 - Thursday 9 A.M. Prayer

Watch the interference, something I will not be able to share in this memoir. I told the Lord I can keep a secret. I have to keep my word. I heard the Lord say, "All right let's get back to digging, don't move, dig right here where we left off." I saw a winepress.

The Same Day 3 P.M. Prayer

I just began to weep before God in his presence. He gave (Isaiah 54:17) "no weapon formed against you shall prosper." Then, I knew warfare was on the menu when I came out of these open visions and realms in God. I kept seeing treasure chests on these strings coming up out of the earth.

The Same Day 6 P.M. Prayer

I saw another giant bulldozer digging up new ground in a new spot; I was in another open vision in a deep hole on a rope in a long well. It was deep. I pull the treasure chest up to the earth. I saw an angel pulling up eight treasure chests up to the earth. Then, the Lord spoke to me and said "his supply never runs out, and you will have strings of finances." Then, I saw this tunnel, nothing but water gushing out of it. He gave me access to the keys to the kingdom, and I saw the souls of men.

Day 5 - Friday 9 A.M. Prayer

I heard the Lord say, "You are transitioning into your next level." Often, when God speaks; we think it's for now. He's just giving us a glimpse early, but, when he knows we are ready to go to that next level. It's definitely not without suffering and opposition from the enemy. Then, I started dreaming about formulas, man this was so real it was like I was in a Chemistry class. I kept seeing all of these formulas. I'm telling you God gave me something, I can hopefully share with the world one day.

The Same Day 3 P.M. Prayer

I just layed in his presence then he began to give me some blueprints of some witty invention that absolutely blew my mind. COMING SOON...

The same day 6.p.m Prayer

Again I went to pray in the same spot as always and began to thank God for what he was doing and cry out to God. He said keep digging daughter and I kept digging. A presence filled the room that I have never, I mean never experienced ever before. I was in a heavenly atmosphere and everything shifted.

Day 6 - Saturday 9 A.M. Prayer

I believe it was my day off on Friday, so I was able to go to bed a little early and get a good night's sleep. I woke up and some music was playing, I thought I left the radio on that night or something. As I layed on my bed and listened; then instantly I knew in my spirit what it was. It was the angels from heaven, it was the most beautiful and holy sound you ever wanted to hear. I just listened. It was such a heavenly sound my ears had never heard before.

It was the most beautiful sound your ears could ever hear, it went on and on. The angels sang and sang, and sang, then, they stopped. I was in awe, but I remembered what God had said. The angels wanted to visit me and I would hear sounds from heaven. It was an encounter I will never forget. Then the Lord told me "I'm letting you out of solitary confinement a day early for good behavior." I said glory and man I was glad. The things I experienced within those six days blew me away. When Paul went to the third heavens he couldn't even speak about it. (Atmospheres)

God is just awesome. 2 Corinthians 4:7 "But we have this treasure in this earthen vessel."

I just yearned for more of God in my inner parts and to continue to explore the deep place in him. You will never experience any of it without sacrifice, obedience and suffering. What I experienced for those 6 days was mind blowing, however the Threshing floor went on for the next fifty days, then immediately I received a special invite from God.

A passage

THE SWEET INVITE

When you think about an invitation or being invited somewhere, that person considers you to be someone special, or good for them to even invite you, right? For example, being invited to a party or wedding or any special event is an honor and privilege to be considered. Once you receive the invitation in the mail or a call saying the time and the place and date, you kind of get excited, then you start thinking about what you're going to wear. Have you ever been to an all white party? Have you ever been invited to a spiritual place by God when he says he wants you to be his special guest for the occasion. " Behold I stand at the door and knock, if any man hears my voice and opens the door, I will come into him and will Sup with him and he with me (revelations) 3-20 (The Christian science journal reads and states. Jesus was a guest at Mary and Martha house and shared his rich treasures, then raised Lazarus from the dead. He also was a guest at Simon's house as he ministered to the widow women a sinner scorned and he showed his love and kindness. He went to Peter's house and raised Peter's wife's mother up. In all these instances the power of jesus lay not in the temporal occasion, but in his conviction that he was " The guest of God"

While I was in prayer, I heard these words: I want you to be my special guest. I was excited. Then he would give me instructions on how to get ready and prepare and be mindful of the time, so I wouldn't miss the event. It was such a sweet invite into his glorious presence it blew me away. I'm still learning in depth what all this involves. All I know is that I wanted to come especially if it was an invite from God. I'm reminded of Luke 14-10 but when you're invited, go sit in the low place, so that when he who invited you comes, he may tell you, Friend, move up higher. Then you will be honored in the presence of all who sit at the table with you. It is a privilege when God himself invites you to that special place beyond your imagination. I had never heard anything of that magnitude in my life, okay it may be mediocre to some of you, but for me it was awesome. While in prayer I would be invited in at different times of the day. Oh! when God calls! As I kept coming to the invite, he said to me after a while, I want you to be my permanent guest. All i can say is something special happened to me every time i went to this place. Such an awesome place to be invited to, what an Awe again moment for me. There's so much to God we can't even imagine his infinite wisdom and Glory. What a special invite, it was all God. It's something God sees in you to be a permanent guest. It's priceless. Sometimes I would be invited about 1pm in the afternoon or at 4pm whatever time he said I tried to be there at that time. It felt like I was at my right of passage to my new level being part of his divine will spiritually, again I was fascinated. I was at his feet now. I'm learning every part of him or what my capacity could hold. He blows my mind when he speaks the unbelievable that my mind can't even phantom because he is good and he's God and because of my obedience and dedication in prayer I'm able to hear him. Have you ever wondered or thought that God is not in a box, and we must keep him out, he is a wonder and the mysteries, the unveiled truth he reveals to his servants who obey him. oh, i yearn for his touch and his presence and everything he pours i just want more and more and more. I just can't get enough. This is better than any drug I've ever been addicted to. I was high off jesus.

Then it became so sweet I was in double awe of his glorious majesty and power. I never wanted it to end. It's like a guess that you invite over, and they never want to leave and it has not ended yet. He would prepare me at certain times to decree and declare some things and pray and worship certain and specific times of the hour. Then he begins to reveal things in the heavenlies. The bible says in the book of St john 14-1-2 Let not your heart be troubled ye believe in God believe also in me. In my fathers house there are many mansions. if it were so, i would have not told you i will go to prepare a place for you. I have heard that preached countless times and one day I ask the lord because it would be preached but never explained ever. Is it a house in heaven?

You said mansions and the lord revealed to me and said those are dimensions and portals and open doors. I found myself sitting in some open doors and atmosphere and dimensions in God. It was a place I had never been before and because I was invited and was able to experience some supernatural encounter with God and the angels adored me; they always wanted to come visit, but of course God has to prepare you. Can you imagine Apostle Paul going to the third heavens, Moses going up in the mount for forty days and forty nights having them encounters with God.

The Scroll

TODAY'S CHURCH

I remember falling asleep on the couch one night and I was awakened in the middle of the night and I had a dream about a scroll and the Lord woke me up and told me to grab a pen and some paper and said write in this scroll, and I began to write.

I felt like I was in a trance. I saw Jesus in the sky so clearly he was surrounded by beautiful colors around him. One color was the color of amber. I saw the number 9,000. He said tell my people I'm coming back and to set their house in order. I was trying to make sense of it all then the Lord began to speak. He said to me this is today's church.

He said my preacher has chosen filthy lucre over me. I sent the pandemic that my people might repent but they have waxed worse and worse.

The angel of the lord said to me they preach what sounds good and have not sounded the alarm and have not told people the error of their sinful ways. He said the church is no more normal; it has turned my people from the true and living God. I'm calling for transformation.

He said we must go back and wash our garments. Many that I have called have caused my people to stumble and turn their back on me. He said write and tell them I have been visiting their churches. I've been sitting in the midst. My church has become a doctrine of devils; they must not only preach what sounds good but both sides. Shepherds have lost their desire for me and have led my people astray, surely they are a backslidden people. He said they refuse to come to the heavenly place where i have called them, they refuse to live in a place of peace saith God. The angel of the Lord began to speak again and said there will be a sound in the earth everyone will hear. He said hang the scroll in the temples.

There is a call in the earth for my son and daughters to come, I'm coming back saith God, but first there will be a great famine and anguish in the land.. there will be a great revival in the land

I'm calling my people to be spiritual giants in the earth. He said they choose tradition and religion over my Spirit.

I walk to and fro in the hearts of my people, yet they still have waxed cold and have left their first love. He said to me my church has turned into an entertainment center and show business. They have used their gifts to swindle. I shall remove them and they will never cause my people to error again. He said my prophets whom I have called walk in the spirit of manipulation, they honor me with their lips but their hearts are far from me. He said I walk in the midst of them and the land is full of wickedness. He began to say my rod of correction is in my hand, if they listen and repent I will heal them, but if not judgment begins in the household of faith. He said if they repent I will forgive them and show mercy if not death is at the door.

Chapter 11

IN THE PROMISE NOW

Things began to turn around for me after being sick and going through the things I had been through for the last three years dealing with Covid and coming out of major surgery. God was still in control; he was bringing me into a season of full restoration.

He was restoring me in every aspect of my life. I hear people often say trust God even when you can't trace him. He was enlarging my capacity. He was putting me back together like Humpty Dumpty. I was broken physically and mentally. I'm telling you I was glad to finally begin to feel better and was able to get back to some kind of normalcy in my life. What the enemy meant for bad God worked out for my good.

He was destroying every generational curse he was elevating me into my next dimension. He said he was promoting me. I was at a new level in a new demension. People often say experience is the best teacher when you go through you know for yourself God is the only one that can bring you out.. Have you ever been in some hard places? I learned some things in my lifetime and one is you can't hurry God, what you go through will teach you patience. I went through some of the hardest challenges in the last twenty years but mainly in the last three years.

The Cross Over...

I went to a service one night and a great man of God laid hands on me and prophetically said God said it's not over yet. I fell out under the power of God and while I was laying on the floor under the power of God, I heard the lord say I'm crossing you over tonight.

I knew what that meant. I had crossed over to the promised land and now it was time to go possess the land, but of course the Lord said it's some giants in the land, but I will give you strategies on how to drive them out.

It wasn't too many days later when some instructions came and one of the first things God told me one night laying in bed was to change my phone number and cut off the old friends. I knew I had to obey. He told me that some time ago I ended up giving my number out when God said no. He said to me he didn't want me to be so accessible to people anymore and I understood why, so I knew I had to obey this time.

What I learned on this journey you can't fake being in a spiritual place with God, that's why you have to guard your anointing, this is a suffering way and you must spend time in his word and in prayer. To live in those realms and dimensions in the Spirit it takes sacrifices and consecration with God. The lord said to me if I wanted the new you must cancel out the old because where I'm taking you they cannot go.

He took me to the book of Exodus and reminded me that the old generation died out, never went into the promised land. I had to die out to the old and embrace the new. and instructed me not to cross back over the line and to keep boundaries and when I look back over my personal life, people really could care less about you. I found myself checking on people and pouring into people for years and nobody wasn't pouring or reciprocating it back to me. I'm so good now I've learned to keep moving because this was a God thing man didn't have anything to do with it. God had promoted me and exalted me spiritually, guess who was at the ordination? It was just me and God. He had promoted me to a new level. "The last shall be first and the first shall be last for many be called but few are chosen.

Mathew 20-16. This time around I pray God will put the right people in my life.

I am who God says I am, despite who and what people say I am. I had boundaries now and God said do not cross back over the line. In other words don't look back to old relationships and old things because he was doing a new thing, and he had elevated me to a new place.

I heard the Lord say I have CREDIT with him. Lord, I just Thank You. I'm just excited about what God has done and what he is going to do for me and through me.

This is my season of manifestation. I'm up next my time and my turn. The lord began to open up some doors for me ....It's finally good to have gone through the process of things to be able to get to the promises of God knowing that he is with me and he is such a loving God. If it had not been for the Lord on my side. He has bought me out with the power of his right hand. I remember waking up on a Sunday morning preparing myself to go to service and couldn't really make up my mind what to wear and the Lord said wear yellow today and I obeyed his voice, and then I asked the Lord why the color of yellow and He replied because your (FUTURE IS BRIGHT!) I love how God speaks to me. I just want to prophetically decree if you are reading this memoir your future is bright.

I'm excited for what God is doing in this next chapter of my life because he told me some years back that he was going to rewrite my story.

Chapter 12

THE NEW BIRTH/ NEW BEGINNING

While in prayer I heard the lord say there were two nations in me which meant two babies and that there was a new birth coming. The first thing that came to my mind was the story of Jacob and Esau about the two nations in Rebecca's wound.

We all can relate. We all have experienced a new birth one time or another when we became born again christians. The scriptures say in John 3-3 when Nicodemus asked Jesus a question: How can anyone re-enter back into his mother's womb and be born a second time?

Then Jesus answered and "Verily, truly I tell you, no one can enter the kingdom of God unless they are born of the water and the Spirit" Then the Lord goes on to explain this is not a physical experience but a Spiritual birth in order to see and inherit the kingdom of God. The birth is not visible but a special mechanism that is birthed in the Spirit that only God does; he gives Spiritual gifts and special abilities that enable the people of God to be more effective in a particular calling that God places on and in our lives.

I didn't have a clue about being pregnant again let alone two nations or two babies, what in the world am i giving birth to now, all I know the lord whispered and said to me right after, there was going to be some turbulence, then he showed me in a vision of an airplane flying in the air shaking a bit, not to long after that he said your moving at a good altitude and then it leveled off, then I begin to see the airplane moving at a more aggressive speed. I begin to hear the Lord say I'm taking you to levels and your name shall be great in the earth. Whatever I'm pregnant with I'm sure it will be birthed out for his glory and will edify the kingdom of God.

He said there are platforms and levels I'm taking you to and because you waited and went through the process it's your turn and now it's your time. I encourage you as I come to the end of my writing. Wait on God and let him promote you and take you where you need to go..........Psalm 27-14 "Wait for the Lord; be strong and let your heart take courage; wait for the Lord!"

I admonish you to let God take you through the process of crushing because that's where you will find the OIL SPILL. The anointing is hidden in the process.

(Strategies for Warfare)

Spiritual Codes

1212121212121212121212121221212121212126363636
3636636363636636363636363636898989898898989898
9898989898989898981010111010101010101010101010
1010101010454545454545454545454545454545454545
6116161616484848161616484848614861486148614861481551451414
1514145141514145141451414514149939393939391933939139
3913939919393913939181488148814881481488148814881
488148814893993939393939393939393939393939393939
5555555555555555555555555555555555559249249249
249249249259249249249249249249961486148614861486148
6148614861486148614891491491491491491491491491949
14914914919369360360369369369369369369369369369

The First open Visions i seen

It was one night laying in bed early mid-morning about 5:am and the Lord showed me this and I began to write. I went to Rome by the Spirit in a vision and i seen the the Vatican and i seen a ball on a chain with spikes on it and i seen the angel of the Lord swing that ball and chain with the spikes on it like you see in the olympics and it grabbed a hold of that dome and pull the top of it off. The Lord said to me he is going to destroy the works and the spirit of religion.

The second open vision

I saw the rebuilding of the white house brick by brick, the Lord showed me in Los Angeles California the end times preparing for the man of sin. I saw this huge fly that imitated the symbol of the American eagle, then I saw a huge stargate right in the middle of Los Angeles inside where a lot of information was stored where they could see the entire world and what was going on all social media platforms like it was an Information control center. The Lord took me years into the future, something significant about 2024 he said there will be an outbreak in medicine cures coming to the earth. He also said a great revival will happen. He said he was pulling back the curtain of heaven and releasing his healing angels on the earth.

Third open Vision

I was sitting in a chair and I saw a missile come through my window and it was so close to me and I asked the Lord what that was and why was the missile so close he said to me world world three was near.

Fourth open Vision

I saw storms in the south, fierce storms, Hurricanes in diverse places, I saw an Invasion coming to the United States of America. I saw new technologies. The Lord showed me tsunamis and Thailand under water. I asked God why in the vision he said because they are like unto a sodom and gomorrah I saw Atlanta Ga.flooding.. God said we must prepare with food and water.

Fifth open Vision

I was at a service one evening for prayer and while I was on the altar God took me in a vision and i begin to see China and what I saw was in the market places buckets of blood and I saw blood in the walkways, then all of a sudden I saw thousands of people on their knees repenting to God. God said beforehand he was cleansing the earth spiritually and naturally. A Bishop told me that every twenty one years the earth goes through a natural cleansing.

The sixth open Vision

The lord took me up in a vision and I began to see the glaciers melting, malfunctioning in the airplanes. Airlines closing down. Something was going to happen in the netherlands. I saw huge oil spills. I saw a huge crack in the ocean floor. My spiritual daughter one day said she had a dream. It was a crack in the grand canyon. The Lord spoke to me and said it was a crack in the earth's atmosphere and what was, will no longer be. I saw historical monuments crumbling down. I saw Mount Rushmore crumbling. I saw the Statue of Liberty falling over.

I began to see major blackouts, I saw the white house crumbling systems are changing. I saw a firmament of water being released. I saw the pipeline bursting and I saw more train derailments. God said to me watch the middle east. God took me up into another vision and this is what I saw. I was sitting in the desert in Egypt in a chair and saw the pyramid melting like quick sand and the sand was no longer brown, it turned to blood. I saw more tornadoes and strong winds coming.

Sandra Kaye Blue

About The Author

 **Sandra K. Blue** is the loving mother of three amazing children and grandmother of eight adorable grandchildren. She was born October 29, 1963, to the late Sante Holton and Alma D. Blue in Cleveland, Ohio, where she was also raised.

She gave her life to the Lord in 1989 and joined the Greater Love Temple Ministry, in Dover, Delaware under the leadership of Bishop C.I. Bordley, where she served for 11 years.

In 2000, she joined Rivers of Living Water Ministry and served for nine years under the Leadership of Overseer Jonathan Locus Sr. then served under Bishop Phillip Jones for two years where she was affirmed as a minister and there received her Minister license. It was under Bishop Julia Shaffer where she received the call of God by God to the office of a prophet one afternoon in prayer.

Sandra is a stimulating and enthusiastic minister of God with exciting years of prophetic, ministry leadership, and outreach experience. She is a devoted soul winner and loves helping others find Christ and has practically led folks from all backgrounds of life to Christ. Her first passion is intercession, ministering through prophecy, and inspiring others to fulfill their God given purpose.

Ordained and licensed as a minister of the gospel, Sandra is an inspirational writer, prophet, and mentor. She is the founder and owner of BIG. (Because It's God). A firm that specializes in film production! Sandra enjoys the prophetic and sees herself as the modern-day mouthpiece of God revealing the heart of God through prophecy, preaching, and teaching of the Word of God.

Although Sandra studied film at Cleveland State University, the Lord led her into full-time service in the ministry of the Lord Jesus Christ. She is currently working on her first documentary film as a Producer, Director, and Writer through her own company BIG.

Prophetess Blue loves God wholeheartedly and enjoys writing, playing the piano, traveling, and spending time with her grandchildren. As she continues her journey her earnest desire is to be used by God and to hear God say "Well done my good and faithful servant enter into the joy of the Lord"

Prophetess Sandra Blue is available for speaking engagements and Ministry Assignments:

Email: Bigmedia57@yahoo.com

Website: www.becauseitsgod.com

Stay connected on social media

Phone (440) 454-1830

Facebook: Big

Instagram: Imbigperiod

www.ingramcontent.com/pod-product-compliance
Lightning Source LLC
Chambersburg PA
CBHW062006180426
43198CB00037B/2552